Catherine of Braganza

Charles II's Restoration Queen

Catherine
of Braganza

Charles II's Restoration Queen

Sarah-Beth Watkins

Winchester, UK
Washington, USA

First published by Chronos Books, 2017
Chronos Books is an imprint of John Hunt Publishing Ltd., Laurel House, Station Approach,
Alresford, Hants, SO24 9JH, UK
office1@jhpbooks.net
www.johnhuntpublishing.com

For distributor details and how to order please visit the 'Ordering' section on our website.

Text copyright: Sarah-Beth Watkins 2016

ISBN: 978 1 78535 569 1
978 1 78535 570 7 (ebook)
Library of Congress Control Number: 2016946108

A CIP catalogue record for this book is available from the British Library.

Cover image © National Portrait Gallery, London

Design: Stuart Davies

Printed and bound by CPI Group (UK) Ltd, Croydon, CR0 4YY, UK

We operate a distinctive and ethical publishing philosophy in all
areas of our business, from our global network of authors to
production and worldwide distribution.

CONTENTS

Books by Sarah-Beth Watkins

The Tudor Brandons
Lady Katherine Knollys: The Unacknowledged Daughter of
King Henry VIII
Ireland's Suffragettes
Margaret Tudor, Queen of Scots: The Life of
King Henry VIII's Sister

Books for Writers:
Telling Life's Tales
Life Coaching for Writers
The Lifestyle Writer
The Writer's Internet

Chapter One

From Portugal to England
1638–1662

Ribeira Palace was a maelstrom of activity. The English fleet had been spotted arriving in the bay of Lisbon and the exciting news echoed around its halls. Long awaited, this was the moment when Catherine of Braganza knew her destiny was to be fulfilled. Her mother, Donna Luiza, had always sworn to her that she would become Queen of England and today as the court prepared to receive its English visitors and arrange for the departure of their Portuguese princess, Catherine knew she would soon be on her way to wed her new husband, Charles II, England's restoration king.

Whilst Charles had spent the past tumultuous years trying to return to England and his crown, Catherine had led a quiet and secluded life. From the time of her birth at the ducal palace of Villa Viçosa near Evora on the 25th November 1638, Catherine had rarely been at court or been taken outside the palace walls. Yet in 1640, at just two years of age, she was held in front of her father, the Duke of Braganza, in a bid to force his decision on a monumental turning point in Portugal's fortunes.

Portugal was a prosperous trading nation famous for its breakthrough sea voyages, including the discovery of Brazil, and its command of major trade routes. Yet a succession crisis occurred when the young King Sebastian I of Portugal died at the Battle of Alcácer Quibir in 1578 without his body being found. Leaving no heir to take his place, there was no clear successor to the Portuguese crown. His uncle, Cardinal Henry, acted as regent until 1580 when several claimants, including Catherine's great grandmother, began to assert their right to the throne. Amidst the chaos that ensued, Spain declared war on Portugal and Philip II of Spain took control of the country. It would be sixty years later that a man would rise to the challenge of taking back Portugal from Spanish rule. That man was Catherine's father.

Now on her second birthday the Duke of Braganza, was being urged to assert his claim to the throne. Dom Gaspar Coutigno, envoy for all the Portuguese nobles who had tired of Spain's tyrannical rule, pressed the duke to be their figurehead and support their bid to take back their country, but the duke wavered. He was a placid man, content with his lot. He owned estates that comprised a third of the kingdom and was happy to spend his time in the countryside away from the politics and intrigue of the capital. But Donna Luiza, Catherine's mother, had other ideas. Spanish by birth, she was determined the family she had married into should assert its right to reign and the duke become crowned king of Portugal. As he continued to prevaricate, she ordered her ladies to fetch their daughter, telling the duke 'Today our friends are gathered round us to celebrate the birthday of our little Catherine. Who knows but that this new guest may have been sent to signify the will of heaven, through especial grace, to invest you with the crown of which you have been so long deprived by Spain?' When Catherine was brought to her Donna Luiza held her up to the duke for his kiss and said 'How can you find it in your heart to refuse to confer the rank of a king's daughter upon your child?'[1] That small kiss changed the duke's mind and he agreed to the rebellion.

Dom Gaspar rode fast for Lisbon to proclaim the duke as King João IV of Portugal. Alerting the rebel nobles to his success, the freedom of the capital and country commenced. The palace was taken by force, the Spanish Secretary of State, Vasconcelles, was slaughtered and the Spanish Vice-Queen was secured, forced to give orders for the town's armed fortress to surrender. Once the city was under control, the Archbishop of Lisbon rode through the city to tell the people they were free from Spanish rule and now had their own king.

King João wasted no time in heading for Lisbon once he had heard it had been captured in his name and the people welcomed him with open arms. Bonfires blazed, bells rang out and firework displays coloured the sky. Portugal had been liberated, but for the new king it would be no easy conquer with years of skirmishes and attempted assassinations.

Whilst her father was concentrating on ruling his reclaimed kingdom, Catherine was growing into an attractive young woman with 'her mother's Spanish complexion and dark eyes and hair',[2] but being educated at a convent where her seclusion was complete. It was even rumoured that she would become a nun and embrace religious life although she knew that her mother had other plans for her. In 1661, Maynard wrote of her as 'not having been out of the palace in five years, and hardly ten times in her life'.[3] Her eventual return to the palace coincided with the death of her beloved father in 1656.

In King João's will, Catherine was left the 'island of Madeira, the city of Lanego, and the town of Moura, with all their territories, rents, tributes and other privileges'[4] but only on the proviso that she married within the kingdom. Catherine's mother, the formidable Donna Luiza, had no intention of letting this happen. Her sights were firmly on the exiled Charles Stuart, who she was certain would one day return to English shores. And Luiza now had the authority to begin pushing this union forward. Her eldest son Alphonso, although now proclaimed king, was not yet of age to take the crown and he had also suffered an illness at the age of three that left him paralysed on his left side and mentally unstable. He spent his days rabble-rousing with his friends, causing his mother great concern for his future. But for now she was regent and could further her daughter's marriage.

The idea of marriage between Catherine and Charles had been broached as far back as 1644 when Donna Luiza had contacted the fated King Charles I regarding the marriage of his son and the uniting of England and Portugal. At the time Charles I did not consider his son's marriage to a Catholic princess advisable and Luiza's proposal went no further. But she had never given up on the idea, determined as she was, and watched on as the fortunes of the Stuart kings waxed and waned.

Donna Luiza bided her time and when it seemed that the restoration of Charles II was imminent she contacted General Monck, the man who would see Charles back from exile and restored to the throne, about a possible match. Whether he gave it any consideration or passed her proposal on to Charles is not known. Charles was in Breda at the time and hotly pursuing Princess Henriette Catherine of Orange-Nassau. His thoughts of marriage only revolved around this delightful princess but his proposal was turned down and events overtook the young exile. His country was anxious for his return.

Charles had fled to Europe two years after his father, Charles I was executed. In vain he had tried to regain his father's crown but after his defeat at the Battle of Worcester by Cromwell's New Model Army, he spent the next nine years impoverished and homeless waiting for the day he could return to England. That day came on 25th May 1660, when he answered the call of a new Parliament convened after Cromwell's death and the abdication of his son Richard as Lord Protector, and took ship from Breda to Dover. General Monck who had aided his restoration was the first to greet him back on English soil.

On his 30th birthday, 29th May, Charles rode into London on horseback, flanked by his two brothers, James and Henry, past General Monck and his 30,000 strong army gathered on Blackheath. At Deptford they were greeted by the Lord Mayor of London who offered Charles the sword of the capital and was immediately knighted. Charles continued towards Whitehall, a journey that took him seven hours, 'surrounded by a crowd of the nobility, with great pomp and triumph and in the most stately manner ever seen, amid the acclamations and blessings of the people...The mayor and magistrates of the city met him and tendered the customary tributes, and he passed from one end to the other of this very long city, between the foot soldiers who kept the streets open, raising his eyes to the windows looking at all, raising his hat to all and consoling all who with loud shouts and a tremendous noise acclaimed the return of this great prince so abounding in virtues and distinguished qualities of every sort'.[5]

Once at Whitehall, Charles continued to greet his people and the city continued to celebrate his arrival. The Venetian ambassador reported 'For three days and three nights they have lighted bonfires and made merry, burning effigies of Cromwell and other rebels with much abuse. The foreign ministers have taken part in these rejoicings, and I also, in addition to the illuminations have kept before the door a fountain of wine and other liquors, according to the custom of the country, much to the delight of the people and amid acclamations'.[6]

As Donna Luiza had been convinced he would, Charles had returned to his kingdom and she could continue her plans to marry Catherine off to the English king. High on the tide of his homecoming, for the moment a wife was far from Charles' mind. He had the nineteen-year-old Barbara Palmer to warm his bed and it was rumoured she had been by his side from his very first night at Whitehall. It is not known when Charles first met Barbara, a woman who would feature in his life for a long time to come, but one suggestion is that she was used to take messages to the exiled king in Breda. Her father, Lord Grandison, had been a staunch Royalist and supporter of Charles I and she had married another Royalist, Roger Palmer, in 1659 who donated £1000 to Charles' cause. But this auburn-haired, blue-eyed beauty was no saint. She had been the lover of the Earl of Chesterfield before her marriage and continued the affair long after. Her relationship with her husband was one of convention and her focus now was on being the king's mistress. The first few months of Charles' reign were tumultuous and Barbara was his comfort and nightly companion. She was his support through the death of his younger brother Henry in September and his sister Mary of Orange in December, both to smallpox. Charles' other brother James, Duke of York, was also cause for concern but of an entirely different nature.

James had made a trip to the Netherlands to visit their sister Mary, Princess of Orange. While there he met Anne Hyde, his sister's maid of honour, and the daughter of Charles' chancellor, Sir Edward Hyde. Not only was she now pregnant but James and Anne had married in secret on 3rd September. Hyde, soon to become Lord Clarendon, was a staunch Royalist and had accompanied Charles into exile in Jersey. In gratitude for his service the king had given him the position of Lord Chancellor in 1658 before his return and looked upon him as one of his chief advisers. Both the king and his lord chancellor were then horrified to find out what had happened without their knowledge. James panicked and tried to get out of the marriage by saying that the child Anne Hyde carried could be anybody's. Understandably her father was furious both at James' slander and the position his daughter had put him in. Charles decided to calm the situation and declared that James had married the girl and married to her he would stay.

Henrietta Maria, their mother, had other ideas. The indomitable dowager queen who had supported Charles I throughout the English Civil War had now made her home back in France. She was furious when she heard that James had married beneath him and, packing her travelling trunks, swore she was off to England to 'marry the King, my son, and try to unmarry the other',[7] and to prevent 'so great a stain and dishonour to the crown'.[8] But there was nothing she could do about James. His marriage had been declared valid and Anne Hyde was now the Duchess of York. Charles, however, was another matter.

The Portuguese ambassador and Catherine's godfather, Francisco de Mello, was working hard to ensure that the next queen would be Catherine of Braganza and the Catholic Henrietta Maria supported the match, as did her patron, Louis XIV, king of France, who felt it advantageous that Portugal be linked with England rather than any other nation. France had long been at war with Spain themselves but had recently signed a peace treaty with them. Still, there was no love lost with Spain and Louis supported the Portuguese marriage over all others.

De Mello began by seeking an audience with the Lord Chamberlain, the Earl of Manchester suggesting 'that there was in Portugal a princess in her beauty, person, and age, very fit for... (the king)... who would have a portion suitable to her birth and quality. She was indeed a catholic, and would never depart from her religion, but she had none of that meddling activity which sometimes made persons of that faith troublesome, when they came into a country where another mode of worship was practised; that she had been bred under a wise mother, who had carefully infused another spirit into her, and kept her from affecting to interfere in state affairs with which she was totally unacquainted, so that she would be contented to enjoy her own religion, without concerning herself with what others professed'.[9]

The Lord Chamberlain, after discussion with Charles, sent for the Portuguese ambassador to address the king with terms for such an arrangement. Catherine's dowry was put forward: £500,000, the possession of Tangier and Bombay, plus free trade with Brazil and the East Indies. Portugal was wealthy and England desperately needed money. It was an appealing proposal. An impressed Charles consulted with his chancellor Clarendon who objected to Catherine on the grounds that she was Catholic and advised him to take a Protestant wife to which Charles replied that he was unlikely to find one.

These sentiments were reiterated again at a secret council meeting to which only the Duke of Ormonde, the Lord Treasurer, the Lord Chamberlain, Secretary Nicholas and, of course, Clarendon were invited. Charles began by explaining he had consulted his two naval captains, Lord Sandwich and Sir John Lawson, as to the whereabouts of Tangier. He had never heard of it before – would it really be of any benefit for England to own such land? His captains felt that it would indeed be a good acquisition and it was better to be in English hands rather than the Dutch, but really would Charles still not consider a Protestant wife and perhaps a German one? Charles retorted negatively 'Oddsfish! They are all dull and foggy! I cannot like any one of them for a wife!'[10] A mention of his old flame the Princess Henriette Catherine of Orange-Nassau incensed him further and so it was agreed that of the Catholic princesses in Europe, Catherine was the best choice.

Francisco de Mello was informed and Charles supplied him with two ships to return to Lisbon to share the good news with Catherine's mother and brothers. Such was the rejoicing in the royal court of Portugal that the ambassador was rewarded for his negotiations with the title of Conde de Ponte. Donna Luiza was delighted that all her machinations had resulted in agreement to the marriage of her daughter to the king of England. The Portuguese ambassador was asked to return forthwith and conclude the arrangements – no easy voyage – but on his return to England, he found the mood at court had changed and Charles would not yet agree to meet him.

There were factions at court who still wished to dissuade Charles from his alliance with Portugal. The Earl of Bristol had recently been at the Spanish court and on hearing that Charles may marry a Portuguese princess, he rushed to tell the Spanish ambassador, Vatteville, who was horrified that the king would join forces with Spain's old foe. He remonstrated with Charles but on getting nowhere began to cast slanderous aspersions about the young princess. She was deformed, suffered from bad health and all in Spain knew she was barren. There were also rumours that Lord Chancellor Clarendon was persuading the king to marry Catherine because he'd also heard she was barren which meant his grandchildren, by the Duke and Duchess of York, would inherit the throne.

Vatteville made a suggestion. Why not marry an Italian princess? There were two in Parma he could choose from. Charles actually considered this suggestion and sent the Earl of Bristol off to find out more about them. He was waiting for Bristol's return when the Portuguese ambassador arrived back at court and so he made him wait until he heard Bristol's unflattering report; one was extremely fat, the other 'so ugly that he dared not go forward with any negotiation'.[11] The Spanish ambassador, on seeing that Charles' mind would not be changed, swore that Spain would give the king a dowry to match Catherine's if he would only marry a Protestant bride. Failing that if he continued on his cause, Spain would have no option but to declare war on England. Charles had had enough of being dictated to, he had decided to marry Catherine, and he told Vatteville, who had kept threatening to leave, he was most welcome to and that he 'would not receive orders from the Catholic King (of Spain) how to dispose of himself in marriage'.[12]

Around this time, the King Louis of France also sent Charles a letter supporting the marriage 'as the infanta was a lady of great beauty and admirable endowments, and that he had formerly serious thoughts of marrying her himself'.[13] If Charles had any doubts now they were further dispersed by the arrival of a miniature of Catherine showing her natural beauty; a young, slender face with dark eyes and her brunette hair curled in waves, was to his taste. He remarked 'This person cannot be unhandsome!'[14] and sent for poor de Mello, who had been patiently waiting and worrying, to finalise the marriage arrangements.

Although the negotiations were a court secret, people were starting to wonder. Rumour was rife over who the king would choose for a bride. Pepys, the infamous diarist, recorded on Valentine's Day 1661 that 'the talk of the town now is, who the King is like to have for his Queen'.[15] Just days afterwards Barbara Palmer, the king's mistress, gave birth to his daughter, Anne. Or, she said her daughter was the king's. It could have been her lover's or even her husband's and both Charles and Roger Palmer acknowledged the child as their own. Barbara may have had her hooks into the new king but the merry monarch still needed a wife.

The city was triumphant in its celebration on 23rd April for Charles' coronation. Two weeks after, Charles announced his marriage to Catherine of Braganza to Parliament saying 'I can now tell you, not only that I am resolved to marry, but whom I am resolved to marry. If God please, it is with the daughter of Portugal...And I will make all the haste I can to fetch you a Queen hither, who, I doubt not, will bring good blessings with her to me and you'.[16] But it would be a while yet before Catherine landed on English shores.

De Mello received a state visit from Clarendon and wrote to Catherine's brother, King Alphonso:

Senhor, — This day the grand chancellor came to see me with great pomp, two of his gentlemen bearing his insignia, which are a gilded mace and a crimson velvet purse, embroidered with the arms of his majesty of Great Britain, and this visit is much to be valued, because it has not hitherto been made to any other ambassador. He brought me the resolutions which had been come to by the two houses of lords and commons, copies of which accompany this letter, whereby your majesty will perceive the general approbation which all England shows at the wise choice which this prince has made of the most serene lady infanta, to be queen of these kingdoms. God prosper his actions, and guard the royal person of your majesty, as your vassals desire and have need of.[17]

The marriage treaty was signed on 22nd June 1661 at Whitehall by de Mello, Clarendon and other chief nobles. It stated that Catherine as a Catholic would have freedom of worship and the power to have a private chapel in any palace she resided in as well as giving her an allowance of £30,000 a year. Bombay was to become England's first possession in the East Indies and Lord Sandwich would be sent to take Tangier and then sail on to fetch the Portuguese princess. It was all amicably agreed upon, yet the news infuriated the Spanish ambassador. Vatteville, who hadn't taken the hint and was still in the country, was caught throwing seditious papers out of a window on to passers-by. It was his final act in England. Charles refused to see him to hear his apology and had him forcibly removed from English shores.

Unusually there was no proxy marriage. For Charles as a Protestant marrying a Catholic he would need dispensation from the pope. Not only that but Rome did not recognise Catherine's late father as the King of Portugal, only as a duke, thus making Catherine little more than a duke's daughter and not the princess she actually was. It made no difference to either party. England recognised the sovereignty of Catherine's family and that was all that mattered.

On 30th June, de Mello was summoned to Whitehall, wined and dined and asked to return to Lisbon to ready the princess for her departure to England. He carried with him letters Charles had written in Spanish both to Donna Luiza and to Catherine. His letter to Catherine read:

My Lady and Wife, — Already, at my request, the good count da Ponte has set off for Lisbon; for me, the signing of the marriage has been great happiness; and there is about to be despatched at this time after him, one of my servants, charged with what would appear necessary; whereby may be declared, on my part, the inexpressible joy of this felicitous conclusion, which, when received, will hasten the coming of your majesty. I am going to make a short progress into some of my provinces; in the meantime, whilst I go from my most sovereign good, yet I do not complain as to whither I go; seeking, in vain, tranquillity in my restlessness; hoping to see the beloved person of your majesty in these kingdoms, already your own; and that, with the same anxiety with which, after my long banishment, I desired to see myself within them; and my subjects desiring also to behold me amongst them, having manifested their most ardent wishes for my return, well known to the world. The presence of your serenity is only wanting to unite us, under the protection of God, in the health and content I desire. I have recommended to the queen, our lady and mother, the business of the count da Ponte, who, I must here avow, has served me, in what I regard as the greatest good in this world, which cannot be mine less than it is that of your majesty; likewise not forgetting the good Richard Russell, who laboured on his part, to the same end.

The very faithful husband of your majesty, whose hands he kisses,

Charles Rex.[18]

Catherine replied to Charles 'I give myself reciprocally with you much joy, and could find it in my heart to give it over and over to Your Majesty'[19] and told him it was her greatest desire to be with him but still she had to wait. Winter was approaching and her mother could not let her sail from Portugal into the treacherous waters of the Bay of Biscay. But with the marriage treaty formally ratified, she could now attend court as Queen of England and was seen more publicly in Lisbon than she had been in years. She spent the winter months waiting for the English fleet to arrive, gazing at a miniature of Charles that Sir Richard Fanshawe, the king's ambassador to Portugal, had presented to her and learnt a little English in preparation for her move to her new country.

Charles meanwhile began to make arrangements for the new queen's household at court. Those that had hoped that his mistress Barbara Palmer would soon be put aside were horrified to hear that she was now Lady Castlemaine after the king ennobled her husband. Catherine's ladies needed to be agreed upon and if the king's mistress had a title, she could be included. Lady Suffolk, Barbara's aunt, was given the role of first lady of the bedchamber and in January 1662, Charles' sister, affectionately known as Minette, who was married to the French king's brother the Duc d'Orleans, wrote to him of another lady, Frances Stuart, who would come to feature in all their lives. Minette wrote 'I did not wish to lose this opportunity of writing to you by Madame Stuart, who is taking her daughter to be one of the maids of the Queen, your wife. If it had not been for such a purpose, I can assure you that I should have been very sorry to let her go from here, for she is the prettiest girl in the world and the most fitted to adorn court'.[20] Charles was soon to find out just how appealing she was.

In March, the king told Parliament that he expected Catherine's arrival some time that month and in the meantime he hoped that the London streets, filthy and dung-ridden, would be mended and cleaned before her coming. The Earl of Sandwich had been dispatched to take possession of Tangier, clear the Mediterranean of Barbary pirates and continue on in the *Royal Charles* to collect his new queen. The fleet's arrival in Portugal was timely. The Spanish had been about to attack but after seeing fourteen English men of war ships entering the bay of Lisbon decided against it.

Portugal was in a celebratory mood. Dom Pedro de Almeida, the comptroller of the Portuguese royal household, was sent out in a luxurious barge to welcome the Earl of Sandwich who saluted his coming with the firing of twenty-seven guns. The next day, the earl received a state welcome as he left the *Royal Charles* and journeyed by a coach drawn by six horses and surrounded by heralds, trumpeters, pages and gentlemen into Lisbon to meet Catherine's brother, the young King Alphonso.

He was given sumptuous apartments to stay in courtesy of the Marquez Castello Rodrigo and two days later he finally met Catherine and her mother. At their audience he presented the new queen with the gentlemen who would be members of her household and a gift from Charles, dresses, tailored in the more fashionable English style than the traditional Portuguese farthingales that were seen as outdated in England.

In the days that followed, there were many festivities, bullfighting, firework displays, fetes and carnivals, but the celebrations were marred for the Earl of Sandwich when Donna Luiza put him in an awkward position. She explained to him that there was an issue with Catherine's dowry. Much of it had been spent on the ongoing war with Spain and she could only provide half but assured him the rest would be paid within a year. What could the earl do? Charles and England's treasury wanted and needed that coin. He couldn't return without it but Tangier had already been taken and he could hardly break off the marriage and leave Portugal without Catherine. He had to agree to Donna Luiza's terms but as the ships were being readied to once again set sail he realised that bags of sugar and spice were being loaded instead of any money. Donna Luiza explained she would send her man Diego Silvas with the cargo to obtain a good price for it all in London that would provide Charles with the coin he needed. It was a further blow but by now it was too late to do anything other than take it all back to England.

The day chosen for Catherine's departure was 23rd April, St George's Day – the patron saint of both England and Portugal. Catherine walked at the head of the procession from the Queen's antechamber through the palace to the Hall of the Germans, closely followed by her two brothers, King Alphonso and Dom Pedro. Donna Luiza came to take her leave and when Catherine asked permission to kiss her mother's hand, it was refused. As Queen of England, Catherine no longer had to make this obeisance to the Queen Regent of Portugal. Instead her mother clasped her in a firm embrace but no tears were shed. It would be unseemly to betray their emotions. Her brothers led her to a waiting coach where she turned and curtsied to her mother and then began the long procession down to the quay through a Lisbon awash with celebration and streets lined with well-wishers, and entertainment laid on by musicians and dancers. The Portuguese royals made one stop at the cathedral for a benedictory mass before making their way down to the bay where the English fleet lay waiting for their arrival.

Catherine was taken by barge to the *Royal Charles* accompanied by her chief ladies, the Countesses Penalva and Pontevel and her old friend, Francisco de Mello, who had arranged her marriage, and was now further entitled the Marquez de Sande for his efforts. In other boats were carried her entourage of around one hundred men and women including six maids of honour and a mother of maids, 'six chaplains, four bakers, a Jew perfumer and a certain officer, apparently without employment, calling himself her highness's barber'[21] for only he could style her hair in the outmoded Portuguese fashion.

As Catherine boarded the *Royal Charles* the fleet fired a salute which was answered by the forts on land. Her brother King Alphonso conducted her into the care of the Earl of Sandwich who led her to her appointed cabin where comfortable furnishings awaited her. They were described in a poem published after her marriage:

Her royal cabin and her state room too,
Adorned with gold and lined with velvet through;
The cushions, stools, and chairs, and clothes of state,
All of the same materials and rate;
The bed, made for her majesty's repose,
White as the lily, red as Sharon's rose.
Egypt nor isles of Chittim have not seen
Such rich embroideries, nor such a queen;

Windows, with taffaties and damask hung,
While costly carpets on the floor are flung;
Regions of perfumes, clouds of incense hurled,
In every room of this our little world;
Here she begins her progress, comes aboard,
Turns voyager, to greet her dearest lord.
The royal Charles by sea and land she'll take,
Both for her zenith and her zodiac.[22]

But Catherine was anxious about leaving her home and so rushed back on deck to watch as her brothers sailed back to shore. Her nervousness was exacerbated by the news that she would not yet leave for England. The weather had turned and it was not safe to leave harbour. Impatiently, Catherine paced her sumptuous cabin but an impromptu water carnival was arranged for that evening 'to divert the grief of the royal voyager at her separation from her country and kindred'[23] and it gave her some comfort and distraction. Still the next day a fierce wind blew into the bay and Catherine had to stay in her confines. Her brothers arranged a musical diversion for her in the evening and rowed out to the *Royal Charles* with musicians in tow to serenade her with guitars and viols, singing sonnets, carols and madrigals in honour of her nuptials.

On the morning of the 25th April 1662, all was ready at last, the wind had died down and the *Royal Charles* set sail for England. As soon as Catherine was gone, King Alphonso decided it was time for him to reign instead of his mother. He had reached his majority in 1661 and now wanted Donna Luiza out of the palace but Catherine knew nothing of this as she sailed away from the land of her birth to her new life.

It was not to be an easy crossing. Catherine and her ladies suffered from sea sickness as they were tossed about on the stormy waves. The ladies were also causing issues. They wouldn't sleep in beds that men had slept in, which would be every one given it was a naval ship, and they argued with Catherine about whether she should wear English dresses which they found wholly inappropriate. They sailed through the storm for thirteen days until Mounts Bay in Cornwall came into sight and they could find shelter. Fireworks and gun salutes echoed a welcome from shore but the ships then had to make their way up the coast to Portsmouth when the weather improved.

Just past the Isle of Wight, the fleet was met by the Duke of York's five frigates and the duke sent a message to ask permission to board the *Royal Charles* and welcome Catherine to England. Catherine replied swiftly that any delay would be painful to her. She was anxious to begin her new life and to place her feet on English soil.

Disregarding her Portuguese ladies, she changed into a white satin dress trimmed with lace, one of the dresses that Charles had gifted her. The duke and his men were shown into the small presence chamber on board where Catherine sat on a throne. James knelt as she rose to greet him and her almoner Richard Russell acted as translator as she spoke a formal welcome in Portuguese. Once the formalities were over they were able to converse in Spanish and the duke passed on a letter from the king to assure Catherine that all was in order for her arrival in Portsmouth. The duke visited her every day as they slowly made their way up the Solent and into harbour. They became well acquainted and James even asked to see her in her Portuguese dress. To please him she donned her farthingale and he told her how charming she looked. Pepys wasn't so sure that she was charming anyone. He reported that 'the Queene hath given no rewards to any of the captains or officers'[24] for their service on the voyage, when in fact she had presented the captain with a collar of gold and money to be distributed among the crew as she disembarked.

For her arrival on 14th May Catherine had changed back into an English-styled dress to meet the Governor of Portsmouth, the local magistrates and dignitaries arrayed to greet her. If she had hoped to be greeted by the king, she was disappointed for he was nowhere to be seen. Even the Countess of Penalva had been unable to accompany her as she was so ill with a fever she had to be left on board the *Royal Charles* but Catherine continued her duties regardless. This was her new life and she wanted to embrace it fully. The one thing she asked for was a cup of tea! Although tea had arrived in England, it was rare anyone drank it and instead she was offered a cup of small ale – not quite the same thing.

The Earl of Sandwich seeing Catherine safely to her quarters at the King's House wrote to Clarendon:

> *The queen, as soon as she came to her lodgings, received my lady Suffolk and the other ladies very kindly, and appointed them this morning to come and put her in that habit they thought would be most pleasing to the king, and I doubt not, but when they shall have done their parts, she will appear with much more advantage, and very well to the king's contentment. She is a prince of extraordinary goodness of disposition, very discreet and pious, and there are the most hopes that there ever was of her making the king and us all happy.*[25]

He also reported that Catherine was in 'very good health' but exhausted from her voyage and probably contracting the same fever that the Countess was suffering from, she took to her bed.

In London, church bells rang out and bonfires burnt in honour of Catherine's arrival but it was remarked that no bonfire was lit at Lady Castlemaine's house. In fact, whilst the king should have been journeying to meet Catherine, he was playing with his pregnant mistress, and 'the King and she did send for a pair of scales and weighed one another; and she, being with child, was said to be heaviest'.[26] The Venetian ambassador more diplomatically reported that Charles was busy with Parliament. 'His

Majesty having decided to set out for Portsmouth on Monday went in the morning to Westminster and entering the House of Lords sent for the Commons and gave his assent to all the bills passed, proroguing the session until the 28th February next'.[27] Both the needs of Parliament and the Lady were delaying Charles' journey to meet his new queen.

De Mello, the Marquez de Sande, was fuming at the delay. He had not expected the king to keep his new wife waiting. It was important that this marriage went smoothly. Catherine was recovering from her illness and the voyage but where was the king? Charles began his journey down to Portsmouth after dining with Lady Castlemaine on the 19th May. Travelling in the Duke of Northumberland's coach he was accompanied by his cousin, Prince Rupert of the Rhine, and escorted by a troop of guards. Changing coach at Kingston, they reached Guildford around midnight to spend the night and rest the horses before arriving in Portsmouth around 2pm on the 20th. The Marquez greeted the king in the courtyard of the King's House, relieved he would soon meet Catherine, but was further disgruntled when Prince Rupert pushed him out of the way to walk alongside Charles. Not to be slighted, de Mello called to the king. Portugal and England should walk together – this being an international agreement. Charles took his side and Prince Rupert was asked to move back.

Catherine was still in bed with sickness and the king's first meeting with her took place in her bedchamber. It went well enough with the couple exchanging greetings in Spanish. The king wrote to Clarendon after:

Her face is not so exact as to be called a beauty, though her eyes are excellent good, and nothing in her face that in the least degree can disgust one. On the contrary, she hath as much agreeableness in her looks as I ever saw, and if I have any skill in physiognomy, which I think I have, she must be as good a woman as ever was born. Her conversation, as much as I can perceive, is very good, for she has wit enough, and a most agreeable voice. You will wonder to see how well we are acquainted already; in a word, I think myself very happy, for I am confident our two humours will agree very well together.[28]

Not exactly flushing with compliments, but at least he wasn't turning Catherine away. Given the issue over her dowry and the lack of coin arriving with the fleet, Charles could at this point have refused to continue with the marriage.

Burnet, the preacher and historian, author of a *History of His Own Times* would later say that the Duke of York's friend, Colonel Legge, had heard from the king that he thought Catherine 'a bat instead of a woman'.[29] Burnet is known for his derogatory statements but, true or not, the king seemed pleased enough with his bride-to-be. Lord Chesterfield also commented that Catherine 'is exactly shaped and has lovely hands, excellent eyes, a good countenance, a pleasing voice, fine hair and in a word, is what an understanding man would wish for in a wife'.[30] Mixed opinions, but what they would have agreed on was her devoutness – albeit to the Catholic religion.

On the 21st May 1662 two weddings took place in Portsmouth, one private and one public. Catherine could not see herself as married if the ceremony was not a Catholic one. To this end, there was a secret marriage ceremony in the morning conducted by Lord Aubigny, her almoner. The service was conducted at a little altar in her bedchamber and was attended only by her Portuguese ladies, de Mello and possibly the Duke of York. The public Protestant marriage was then held in the afternoon in the Great Hall of the King's House with the Bishop of London presiding. Catherine wore an English rose-coloured dress covered in little knots of blue ribbon with her hair dressed in curls. The king led her to where two thrones sat beneath a luxurious canopy where the Portuguese ambassador, Sir Richard Fanshawe and Secretary Nicholas waited for them. Formalities were exchanged between Portugal and England and the service was read from the Book of Common Prayer. Catherine made no response either because her English was not good or because the service meant nothing to her – in her heart she had been married in the morning. The bishop pronounced the couple man and wife and a cry of 'Long may they live!' went up. The Countess of Suffolk came forward to cut the little blue knots from Catherine's dress and passed them around as wedding favours, mementoes of the day.

As others continued to celebrate, the king led Catherine back to her bedchamber. Still feeling ill, she tumbled under the covers whilst Charles ordered food to be brought up to them. They dined together before Charles took his leave of his new wife. Catherine could only snuggle down and return to sleep.

Charles wrote to his sister Minette after the wedding to tell her 'I think myself very happy. I was married the day before yesterday but the fortune that follows our family is fallen upon me'.[31] He was referring to consummation of the marriage. Minette had not slept with her husband on their wedding night and Charles also had not slept with Catherine.

Chapter Two

After the wedding
1662-1664

Catherine and Charles left Portsmouth on 27th May, spent one night at Windsor Castle, and arrived at Hampton Court Palace on the 29th – Charles' birthday and the anniversary of his restoration. Pepys, the diarist, had already been to see how Hampton Court was being prepared for the queen. We 'were showed the whole house by Mr. Marriott; which is indeed nobly furnished, particularly the Queen's bed, given her by the States of Holland; a looking-glass sent by the Queen-mother from France, hanging in the Queen's chamber, and many brave pictures'.[1]

Before Catherine could even get as far as her chambers, she had to magnanimously greet all those that had gathered to congratulate her on her wedding; the lord chancellor, judges, counsellors of state, foreign ministers and 'then all the nobility, gentry, and ladies of the court were presented to her, classed, according to their degrees, in different rooms, through which her majesty passed'.[2] Catherine's household had not yet been finalised and the lord chancellor reported that nothing was at all in order except for four dressers and six maids of honour. One of those ladies was the young Frances Stuart who would return from Henrietta Maria's court in France to become one of Catherine's closest companions and also the king's.

Catherine's Portuguese ladies still accompanied her and unfortunately garnered nothing but negative comments 'They are not handsome and their farthingales a strange dress…I find nothing in them that is pleasing'.[3] Evelyn also mentioned their 'monstrous' farthingales and that they were 'sufficiently unagreeable'.[4] For some reason, Catherine had decided to wear her formal Portuguese dress which Evelyn mentions as well as 'she was yet of the handsomest countenance of all the rest, and though low of stature, prettily shaped, languishing and excellent eyes, her teeth wronging her mouth, by sticking a little too far out; for the rest lovely enough'.[5] Not exactly complimentary.

Catherine had time to gather herself after her meet and greet, hopefully with a cup of her beloved tea, before her next audience with the Duchess of York in the evening, who had travelled to Hampton Court along the Thames by barge to greet her new sister-in-law. Over the next few days Catherine would meet even more new faces including the Duke and Duchess of Ormonde, the diarist Evelyn, and the Lord Mayor and Aldermen of London. She was on show as their new queen but also as a novelty and a foreigner. Everything she said and did was watched and commented on. The public were allowed to come and see her eat and were amazed when she used a fork! There were other unusual things that were pointed at including her Indian cabinets and 'much Indo-Portuguese furniture of ebony and blackwood, richly carved, and with twisted columns'.[6] Catherine's Portuguese musicians were also marvelled at but more for their 'very ill'[7] voices.

Catherine had to get used to a more relaxed court than the formal Portuguese one she had come from. She spent a lot of time on her devotions, shutting herself away in her chapel, until de Mello remonstrated with her to relax a little and spend less time on prayer and more time mixing amongst the courtiers. One of her enjoyments was to walk in the gardens and park adjoining Hampton Court Palace along the avenues of lime trees and horse chestnuts and around the flower gardens.

Charles was attentive and courteous for the first six weeks of their marriage. He acted as a devoted new husband should and Catherine responded to him, enjoying his company and accompanying him every evening to the many balls, plays, concerts and entertainments that the court provided, but her happiness wasn't to last.

The strain of her long journey and new marriage caught up with Catherine and she was soon ill again. In June, the Venetian ambassador reported 'the queen, since her arrival in England has suffered from the change, and the damp unsettled weather here. The moment she landed she experienced some derangement of her health, but soon recovered. But she does not eat as she cannot accustom herself to the ways of the country, or drink anything but water, which in England is so much poison, caring little for any diversion as she is of a melancholy disposition, extremely delicate and accustomed to quiet and solitude; disgusted rather than pleased at the confusion of this Court and the crowds of people and new faces constantly coming forward, crowding about and making obeisance, even incommoding her without intermission and without discretion. She has been obliged these last days to confine herself to her apartments and keep quiet owing to another derangement of her health'.[8] Catherine may also have taken to her bed hearing the news that Lady Castlemaine had given birth to the king's son on 18th June.

It is quite possible that Catherine's mother, Donna Luiza, had warned her about the king's mistress before she left Portugal. If not, by now Catherine would surely have heard the rumours. She was content now she was queen and hoped the woman no longer featured in her husband's life, albeit there being a new royal bastard.

Days after his previous report, the Venetian ambassador wrote 'The queen has recovered, to the king's great joy, and now, in perfect health, is beginning to enjoy the delights of Hampton Court. Both their Majesties amuse themselves greatly on the river and other waters that surround that place, in the gondolas sent by your Serenity, which remained idle during the winter cold but are now seen every day and often used'.[9]

Her health may have improved but her peace of mind was soon to be shattered. In July, Catherine's household was still not complete and Charles furnished her with a list of ladies to consider for positions. At the top of the list was Lady Castlemaine. Catherine pricked a pinhole next to all the ladies to show she approved of them, as was the custom, but she destroyed the name of the king's mistress, vigorously scratching it out. Catherine couldn't believe he would even suggest such a thing. A whore in her own household! Charles tried to assure her that his affair was long over but was concerned he owed her family for services rendered to himself and his father in his time. The lady's position in Catherine's household would show his favour. For the first time in their marriage, Catherine shook off her gentle, quiet nature and refused to be convinced. If Charles continued to push for his mistress, ex or not, she would return to Lisbon. Charles was shocked at Catherine's obstinacy. He was used to getting his own way but then so was she. For the moment he had to acquiesce.

Catherine was so used to Charles presenting new people to her that she didn't bat an eyelid when he entered her chambers with yet another new lady on his arm. She didn't hear correctly who exactly this lady was and greeted her accordingly. It was only when one of her Portuguese ladies whispered in her ear that this was in fact the king's mistress, the one and only Lady Castlemaine, that Catherine reacted. Tears welled in her eyes, blood streamed from her nose and she collapsed in a faint. The court was in shock that not only had Charles been brazen enough to introduce his mistress to his queen, as had delighted some of the bawdier courtiers, but Catherine had passed out. What a spectacle!

Charles had no sympathy whatsoever. In fact, he denigrated Catherine for causing such a scene and swore that the only way she could repair the damage was by accepting Lady Castlemaine as one of the ladies of her bedchamber. But Catherine refused. She was absolutely miserable. Her honeymoon period was well and truly over. And while she kept to her rooms, the Lady lorded it up at court, gathering her supporters whilst the queen had only her Portuguese ladies for comfort.

Clarendon, out of a sense of duty, tried to alleviate the situation and remonstrated with Charles over his actions but Charles was infuriated and wanted his queen to see sense. He passionately wrote to his chancellor:

...now I am entered on this matter, I think it very necessary to give you a little good counsel in it, least you may think, by making a further stir in the business, you may divert me from my resolution — which all the world shall never do — and I wish I may be unhappy in this world and in the world to come, if I fail in the least degree of what I have resolved, which is of making my lady Castlemaine of my wife's bed-chamber; and whosoever I find use any endeavours to hinder this resolution of mine (except it be only to myself), I will be his enemy to the last moment of his life. You know how true a friend I have been to you; if you will oblige me eternally, make this business as easy to me as you can, of what opinion so ever you are of; for I am resolved to go through with this matter, let what will come on it, which again I solemnly swear before Almighty God; therefore, if you desire to have the continuance of my friendship, meddle no more with this business, except it be to bear down all false and scandalous reports, and to facilitate what 1 am sure my honour is so much concerned in: and whosoever I find to be my lady Castlemaine's enemy in this matter, I do promise, upon my word, to be his enemy as long as I live. You may show this letter to my lord lieutenant; and if you have both a mind to oblige me, carry yourselves to me as friends in this matter.[10]

Clarendon had to obey his king even though he detested Charles' mistress. He had even forbidden his own wife to receive the Lady but he had to visit Catherine to try to resolve matters. His initial meeting with her ended in tears. Clarendon was an austere and unsympathetic man and his demeanour made Catherine all the more miserable. He went more softly at their meeting the next day asking her how she could have imagined that the king would have waited for his queen without taking a consort. He reminded her that her brothers were no saints in this department either. Catherine agreed with all and seeing her soften, Clarendon went on – 'he came to her with a message from the king, which, if she received, as he hoped she would, she would be the happiest queen in the world; that the king said whatever correspondences he had entertained with other ladies, before he saw her majesty, concerned not her, neither ought she to inquire into them, as he intended to dedicate himself entirely to her; and that if she would meet his affection with the same good humour that she had been accustomed to do, she should have a life of perfect felicity'.[11]

Catherine asked for Clarendon's 'help in returning her thanks to his majesty, and in obtaining his pardon for any passion or peevishness of which she might have been guilty, and to assure him of all future obedience and duty'.[12] She thought the matter was over but Clarendon hadn't finished. To prove her obedience to the king, she must allow Lady Castlemaine to serve her. On that point, Charles would not back down. It was too much. Catherine raged at Clarendon saying once more she would return to Lisbon rather than have that woman in her chambers. Clarendon warned her that her temper would push the king further away. With nothing more to do than report back to his sovereign, Clarendon left Catherine to her rage.

When Charles heard her response, he went at once to Catherine's rooms and there the quarrel raged whilst the court listened on. In the days that followed neither spoke to each other and neither would back down. Clarendon tried once more with Catherine who was now a little remorseful and told him 'that she had been in too much passion, and said somewhat she ought not to have said, for which she would willingly ask the king's pardon on her knees, though his manner of treating her had wonderfully surprised her'.[13] Clarendon asked her if she could honestly keep this up, denying the Lady a place in her chamber 'it was presumed that no wife would refuse to receive a servant that was esteemed and recommended by her husband, and that it was better for her to submit in this instance than that it should be done without her consent'.[14] Catherine listened to the Chancellor's argument and then told him, 'that the king might do what he pleased, but she never would consent to his requisition'. It was a royal stand-off.

Charles' sister, Minette, wrote to him from France, appalled at his behaviour towards his queen. 'I beg you to tell me how the Queen has taken this. Here people say that she is in the deepest distress and to speak frankly I think she has only too good reason for her grief'[15] but Charles was in a vindictive mood and he didn't care what anyone else thought. He railed at Catherine about the non-payment of her dowry, insulted de Mello, the Portuguese ambassador and had Diego Silvas, the man sent to sell the dowry goods, thrown into prison. He also swore that he would dismiss all of Catherine's Portuguese staff. Charles was king and his new queen would learn not to cross him.

The animosity between the royal couple had to abate at some point and it did with the arrival of Charles' mother, Henrietta Maria on 28th July. All the court gathered to greet her at Greenwich Palace. In an effort to be nice to his queen and her entourage, Charles even sent a special carriage to collect the slighted Portuguese ambassador but de Mello sent excuses he was ill – more likely sick at Catherine's mistreatment – and refused to attend.

The formidable Henrietta, whom Catherine had been anxious over meeting, greeted her daughter-in-law with effusive kisses and told her to 'lay aside all compliments and ceremony, for that she should never have come to England again except for the pleasure of seeing her, to love her as a daughter, and serve her as a Queen'.[16] Catherine had found an ally and a much-needed friend. At this their first meeting, Catherine sat at her side whilst

Charles was made to sit on a footstool. The women would have lots to discuss, albeit through a translator as Henrietta didn't speak Spanish and Catherine had little French or English. She was at least able to convey how delighted she was to meet her and 'that, in love and obedience, neither the king or any of her own children should exceed her'.[17]

Charles was on his best behaviour, courteous and attentive, to the two queens in his life. He had his mother fooled early on when she wrote to her sister, Christine, the Duchess of Savoy, 'the queen my daughter-in-law is the best creature in the world who shows me the greatest goodwill, and I have the joy of seeing that she and the king are very much in love'[18] – or perhaps she was just telling her sister what she hoped to hear.

They were at least both making an effort. On the next day Charles had business in the city and Catherine rode out to meet him on his return 'a gallantry which the king so highly appreciated, that he expressed his pleasure most heartily, which was much applauded by the court'.[19]

Henrietta Maria had wanted to return to Somerset House, her previous residence, but it was in the midst of renovation and not yet ready for her. Instead she returned in state to Hampton Court where Catherine welcomed her with open arms. In the days that followed the king's mistress was not seen at court, choosing to spend her time at Richmond, and her cronies acted respectfully towards Catherine. It was a relief for the young queen to spend her time with such an understanding woman as Henrietta, to share their Catholic devotions together and to have a reprieve from her argument with Charles.

And there was much to prepare for. Catherine's state entry into London was on 23rd August 1662. A royal aquatic progress or *Aqua Triumphalis* was organised instead of a coronation presumably as Catherine would not have been happy with a Protestant ceremony. She was carried in a royal barge accompanied by the king, the Duke and Duchess of York, Prince Rupert and his brother Edward and the Countess of Suffolk. Both her ladies the Countesses Penalva and Ponteval were ill and unable to chaperone her. The barge travelled eight miles from Hampton Court before they swopped to a larger river-going vessel with glass windows and a red and gold canopy to take them as far as Putney. There they embarked on the state barge decorated with the royal arms and a canopy of gold brocade. Catherine looked resplendent in a gown of cloth of gold intertwined with silver thread as she took her place beside the king and twenty-four scarlet-clad bargemen rowed them into London.

Evelyn wrote:

I was spectator of the most magnificent triumph that ever floated on the Thames, considering the innumerable boats and vessels, dressed with all imaginable pomp; but, above all, the thrones, arches, pageants, and other representations, stately barges of the lord mayor and companies, with various inventions, music, and peals of ordnance, both from the vessels and the shore, going to conduct the new queen from Hampton Court to Whitehall, at the first of her coming to town. In my opinion, it far exceeded all the Venetian Bucentoras, &c, on the occasion when they go to espouse the Adriatic. His majesty and the queen came in an antique-shaped open vessel, covered with a state or canopy of cloth of gold, made in the form of a high cupola, supported with high Corinthian pillars, wreathed with flowers, festoons, and garlands.[20]

As the aquatic progress made its way to Whitehall, music rang out from the shore and from the gathered river vessels, guns saluted the new queen as she passed along the Thames so tightly packed with boats you could hardly see the water. The people thronged along the riverside, cheering and waving, welcoming Catherine to London. The Queen-Dowager, Henrietta Maria, was waiting for them at a pier built especially for the occasion at Whitehall and as the king and queen disembarked cannons fired a royal salute. The celebrations lasted well into the evening with much feasting and dance.

Catherine's arrival at Whitehall had been magnificent and she was buoyed on the love of her new people and the attentiveness of her king but Barbara was waiting in the shadows. She had watched the queen's state entry and vowed to be back at court soon. She didn't have long to wait. As soon as Somerset House was ready for the king's mother and she had moved to her new surroundings, Barbara was back at Whitehall. Still the argument about her positon hadn't been resolved between king and queen and Charles began to ignore Catherine and pay attention to his mistress once again.

In September, Pepys saw Catherine for the first time at Somerset House sitting to the left of the Queen-Dowager. By this time Lady Castlemaine was also in attendance. Although Henrietta Maria felt for Catherine she was more relaxed when it came to kings and their mistresses. She had grown up with her own illegitimate siblings which her father Henri IV raised as one happy family. Barbara was now a fixture in Catherine's life; one she could not escape but one she could ignore. For Catherine, the first flush of marriage was over. It was plain that Charles preferred his mistress to her and all she could do was act with dignity in the face of adversity however miserable she felt. And there was yet another reminder at court about how much the king valued his mistresses – his first born son. Pepys recalled what he had seen at Somerset House:

Here I also saw Madam Castlemaine, and, which pleased me most, Mr. Crofts, the King's bastard, a most pretty spark of about 15 years old, who, I perceive, do hang much upon my Lady Castlemaine, and is always with her; and, I hear, the Queens both of them are mighty kind to him. By and by in comes the King, and anon the Duke and his Duchess; so that, they being all together, was such a sight as I never could almost have happened to see with so much ease and

leisure. They staid till it was dark, and then went away; the King
and his Queen, and my Lady Castlemaine and young Crofts, in one
coach and the rest in other...[21]

James Crofts was the son of the king and Lucy Walter, his
mistress from way before the Restoration. James had been placed
in his grandmother, the Queen-Dowager's care, when he was
around ten and had grown up with her in Paris – another sign
that Henrietta Maria was as lenient as her son when it came to
mistresses and their offspring.

Pepys went on to say:

The King and Queen were very merry; and he would have made the
Queen-Mother believe that his Queen was with child, and said that
she said so. And the young Queen answered, "You lye;" which was
the first English word that I ever heard her say which made the King
good sport; and he would have taught her to say in English,
"Confess and be hanged"[22]

There were moments when in the presence of others that the king
was jovial and playful with Catherine but they were few and far
between. Catherine was living in a wretched situation. The
women of the court flocked to Lady Castlemaine leaving the
queen to sit alone and neglected, save one or two of her
Portuguese ladies. Catherine had inadvertently made matters
worse when a young priest, Father Talbot, had warned her that
Barbara was an enchantress. Given the connotations of witch-
craft, Catherine had tried to warn the king who took her story to
Lady Castlemaine. Barbara flew into one of her well-known
rages, demanding the priest be removed from court. Catherine
lost support over it, for it was never good to denigrate such a
popular mistress or repeat gossip, and now 'the world so shy of
her that all that had any kindness for her shun her'.[23]

She took to going to bed early whenever Barbara was at court.

Clarendon reported that Barbara followed Catherine as if she was one of her ladies even though Catherine had still not allowed her the role of lady of the bedchamber; 'she thrust herself into the royal coach, and went wherever the queen went – to the park, the theatre, to the houses of the nobility'.[24] There was no peace for Catherine even in her devotions as the king's mistress regularly accompanied her to mass. Following Catherine into her bedchamber one day, Lady Castlemaine was cheeky enough to ask the queen how she had the patience to sit so long 'a-dressing' to which Catherine replied 'I have so much reason to use patience, that I can well bear such a trifle.'[25] The only time Catherine could be rid of her was in the evening when her bedchamber was quiet, by now hardly even frequented by the king. Pepys mentions that Catherine was pregnant in October but it seems implausible given they hardly spent any time with each other. Charles was back to dining with his mistress every night. True, it was both of their duties to produce an heir but their marriage bed was cold whereas Barbara's was warmed every evening.

Catherine was now made all the more miserable by Charles carrying out his threat to send her entourage back to Portugal. It was customary for the original wedding party to be reduced in such a way but to Catherine it just felt like she was losing her family. She had received nothing of the allowance she was due as per her dowry so could not even send her people away with payment for their services. Her dowry was an extremely sore point with Charles. There had been trouble in both Tangier and Bombay and there was still no income from the sugar and spices that Catherine had sailed with. She was left with only the elderly Countess of Penalva who was too decrepit to travel, some kitchen staff and the priests of her chapel.

Catherine just gave up and gave in to Charles' wishes. How could she live such a miserable life when she had been so happy to be marrying England's king and starting a new life in a new country? Perhaps Charles would love her more if she accepted his mistress. She shocked everyone by suddenly acting friendly towards Lady Castlemaine. She 'permitted herself to fall into familiarity with her, was merry with her in public, and spoke kindly of her, and in private used no one more friendly'.[26] A case of if you can't beat them, join them. But for that she was scorned too – her plan backfired. The king thought her deceitful and untrustworthy. How could she have been so fickle as to change her mind? He had no compassion for the sad and lonely queen. He had been coming around to her way of thinking, toying with the idea of putting his mistress aside and now he felt like all the fuss had been for nothing. Clarendon wrote:

this total abandoning her own greatness, this lowly demeanour to a person she had justly contemned, made all men conclude that it was a hard matter to know her, and consequently to serve her. And the king himself was so far from being reconciled by it, that the esteem which he could not hitherto in his heart but retain for her, grew now much less. He concluded that all her former anguish, expressed in those lively passions which seemed not capable of dissimulation, was all fiction, and purely acted to the life by a nature crafty, perverse, and inconstant.[27]

Whatever Catherine did, she could not win. In November, at least her 25th birthday was celebrated with some magnificence. The court poet, Edmund Waller, composed a poem which was sung to her by a Mary Knight.

This happy day two lights are seen,
A glorious saint, a matchless queen;
Both named alike, both crowned appear –
The saint above, the infanta here;
May all those years which Catharine
The martyr did for Heaven resign,

Be added to the line
Of your bless'd life among us here!
For all the pains that she did feel,
And all the torments of her wheel,
May you as many pleasures share!
May Heaven itself content
With Catharine the saint!
Without appearing old,
An hundred times may you,
With eyes as bright as now,
This welcome day behold![28]

Everyone knew of Lady Castlemaine's influence over the king. It was something that Catherine would see over and over again. Even on state occasions Catherine had to watch on as the king's mistress enjoyed herself, flirting and dancing. At a Grand Ball on New Year's Eve, Catherine and Charles entered the ballroom followed by the Duke and Duchess of York and other nobles. Charles immediately took to the dance, leading the Duchess of York onto the floor. The king's son, Crofts, danced with the king's mistress as Catherine watched on yet again, not knowing any of the dances such as the brantle and the coranto, but swearing to herself she would learn them. Lady Castlemaine outshone all the ladies, including Catherine and the duchess, so adorned with jewels was she. Expensive gifts from Charles were ever forthcoming. It was even rumoured that she had made the king give her all the presents he had received over Christmas.

The new year was a lonely one for Catherine. She still suffered the king's displeasure and it was said he didn't dine with her once for the first few months of the year. Lady Gerard tried to remedy the situation by inviting the king and queen to dine with herself and her husband, Lord Gerard of Brandon, later Earl of Macclesfield, but when the king arrived and found his mistress had not been invited, he promptly left for her apartments. The king later dismissed Lady Gerard for slighting Lady Castlemaine and Catherine lost one of the few supporters she had.

On 14th February 1663, Charles' illegitimate son, James Crofts, was created Duke of Monmouth. Catherine had actually grown to like the boy but had hotly opposed his rise in status. To have the king's bastard at court was one thing, to raise him to a dukedom was another. The warrant for his creation spoke of Crofts as the king's 'natural' son and it was an affront to Catherine who hoped to give the king his true heirs. The Duke of York wrote to Clarendon of the royal couple's latest argument, 'My brother hath spoken to the Queene yesterday concerning the owning of his sonne, and in much passion she told him that from the time he did any such thing, she would never see his face more'.[29] But it was all passion and temper which Catherine by now knew wouldn't get her anywhere for Charles went ahead and the Duke of Monmouth was duly created.

As Catherine steamed in her apartments, the king was enjoying his nightly trips to Lady Castlemaine's, where she entertained him. On one evening, she also invited Frances Stuart, Catherine's maid of honour, a childlike and innocent young girl, or at least that is how she appeared, and Charles became quite taken with her. Pepys had heard a delicious rumour that Barbara had put on a mock marriage with Frances – 'at night began a frolique that they two must be married, and married they were, with ring and all other ceremonies of church service, and ribbands and a sack posset in bed, and flinging the stocking'[30] which the king was most delighted with.

The restoration court was a whirl of pleasure and scandal, not for the queen of course, but for all the other courtiers who flocked to the king and his mistress and who drank, gambled and whored every night. Anything went in such licentious and scandalous times and Pepys even reported that at one ball, a Portuguese lady managed to give birth to a baby whilst dancing which was scooped up by the king and then taken to his laboratory for dissection – but then Pepys did love a good rumour.

There was celebration on 20th April 1663 when the now Duke of Monmouth married Anne Scott, daughter of Francis Scott, Earl of Buccleuch. Catherine was gracious enough to make Anne one of the ladies of her bedchamber and at the St. George's day ball at Windsor three days later Catherine led the dancing – something she had been practising for months – with the bridegroom. She had forgiven Charles for making Monmouth a duke but now the king would cause her further affront. As she danced with the young man, the king came up to him, kissed him and made him put his hat on, a disrespectful gesture to the queen from one beneath her. To all that were gathered there it intimated that Charles was going to make Monmouth heir to the crown if Catherine did not produce an heir. Catherine let the matter go this time for by now she was learning how little influence she truly had once Charles had made up his mind.

Their relationship was gradually improving and Catherine didn't want to spoil it. Her love of dance had brought out a lively side to her and Charles responded to his more playful wife writing to his sister Minette 'my wife sends for me just now to dance so I must end'.[31] His change of mood may have been because Catherine was joining in more in court life or maybe it was because he had found another distraction. In May, the King's Company opened a new playhouse, the Theatre in Bridges Street (later the Theatre Royal) which provided evening entertainment for the royals and Charles' first glimpse of Nell Gwyn, the actress.

It may also have occurred to Charles that if he never courted his queen, she would never become pregnant – something Catherine dearly wanted. If she bore Charles' heir it would stabilise her position and best the king's mistresses. In May 1663 Catherine's physician recommended that she take a trip to

Tunbridge Wells to benefit from the reddish waters of the Chalybeate spring, discovered in 1606, known to aid fertility as well as many other ailments. She had yet to receive any of the allowance she was due a year and so sent to the Lord Treasurer for the funds to undertake the journey. She was told since she had already spent her £30,000 allowance there was no coin left available. Catherine hadn't even seen this kind of money. She had been living frugally and her household had cost merely £4,000 to run since her arrival in England. The treasurer responded that wherever the money had gone, it was gone and there was nothing left to give. Catherine knew full well where it was likely to have been spent – somewhere between the king and his mistress – but she could do little but wait for funds to be issued to her.

She heard great news from home in June when the Portuguese defeated Spain at the battle of Ameixial. Catherine was ever anxious of news from her country of birth, a country she was still strongly loyal to. Spain had never stopped trying to conquer Portugal and had overrun the south of the country taking the town of Evora and pressing onwards towards Lisbon but with a combined force of 17,000 Portuguese troops bolstered by 2,000 English men, the Spanish were pushed back and thoroughly defeated. Catherine's brother, King Alphonso, had rewarded the troops with snuff which hadn't gone down too well and Charles made reparation by sending £40,000 over to be shared out amongst the men.

Although money couldn't be found for her trip to Tunbridge Wells, she was delighted that Charles was supporting Portugal and their relationship continued to improve. Pepys noted 'the Queen hath much changed her humour, and is become very pleasant and sociable as any; and they say is with child, or believed to be so'.[32] This is another one of his rumours that isn't confirmed. The royal couple definitely seemed to be spending more time with each other and Lady Castlemaine's influence was waning – for the time being anyway. Catherine and Charles took daily walks in Hyde Park taking in the aviaries along Birdcage Walk or wandering in the Mulberry Gardens and were spotted driving in a coach sitting 'hand in hand'.[33] Catherine looked more relaxed than she had done since her arrival in England, dressed in the fashion of the day and leaving her hair loose and tousled. On 4th July, they reviewed the king's guard, horse and foot, and were accompanied by the king's mother. Lady Castlemaine was nowhere in sight. Pepys noted 'the King is grown colder to my Lady Castlemaine than ordinary, and that he believes he begins to love the Queen, and do make much of her, more than he used to do'.[34] About time, one would think.

But he was also making much of the queen's maid of honour, Frances Stuart 'with her sweet eyes, little Roman nose, and excellent taille'.[35] Catherine was well aware of this new paramour and of plans afoot to make her the king's new mistress. The Duke of Buckingham was no friend to the queen and was related to Lady Castlemaine, with whom he had a tempestuous relationship. He insinuated himself into Frances' good graces and arranged for his sister, the Duchess of Richmond, and his wife to give a party where the king and Frances would be thrown together after an evening of much food and wine. Hearing of such a party, Catherine decided to thwart their plans and arrived with Lady Castlemaine in tow. Whether Frances had asked her to intercede on her behalf or whether Catherine decided to defend her maid's virtue herself, we shall never know, but for now she was safe.

The Duke of Buckingham was not a man to be thwarted and he supported his friend the Earl of Bristol in bringing an impeachment against the Lord Chancellor, Clarendon, that summer, in the House of Lords. One article of the impeachment was an attack on the king's marriage. Somehow rumours of their first marriage – the secret Catholic one – had leaked out. Clarendon was charged with bringing the king and queen together 'without any settled Agreement in what manner the

Rights of Marriage should be performed'[36] and of exposing the king to a 'suspicion of having been married in his own Dominions by a Romish Priest'[37] – an illegal act at the time. Charles was furious and banned Buckingham, Bristol and their co-conspirator, Sir Henry Bennett, from court and instructed the lords to throw the impeachment out. Whether they had had a private service was no concern of theirs, there had been a public Protestant one and the queen was still lawfully his wife. Catherine who must have still worried over her relationship with the king felt great relief at how Charles had defended their marriage. They may have their ups and downs but the king was proving loyal and supportive towards her.

Funds were finally found for Catherine to visit Tunbridge Wells, a little village at the time that was referred to as 'les eaux de scandale'[38] by the French ambassador, known for being a place of romantic liaison. For Catherine, it was a means to an end. She desperately wanted to give the king a legitimate child so each day for a month she took the waters. When that didn't have the desired affect her doctors recommended that she travel to Bourbon in France which would mean months away from the king. Catherine's relationship with Charles was settling down but the last thing she wanted was to leave him to his mistresses for an extended period. One physician, Sir Alexander Fraser, declared that he had analysed the Bourbon waters and found them much the same as at Bath. The court moved with Catherine this time and she and the king took rooms in the Abbey House, a mansion belonging to Dr Pierce, the court physician, whilst the nobles had to find accommodation in the surrounding area. There Catherine took the waters again and hoped that they would give her a much longed for child.

Their stay in Bath was followed with a state visit to Bristol. Catherine and the king were accompanied by the Duke and Duchess of York, Prince Rupert, the Duke of Monmouth and other important courtiers to meet with the mayor and aldermen of the city. A 150-gun salvo sounded their arrival and they were richly entertained at the home of Sir Richard Roger where after dinner Charles knighted four gentlemen and Catherine was given a present of 130 pieces of gold – an extravagant gift and one sorely needed by the impoverished queen.

All too soon it was time to return to Whitehall. Catherine had had a pleasant summer, delighting in the king's attentiveness towards her and she had hoped that this new state of happiness would continue but as soon as the court were back in London, Charles began to visit Lady Castlemaine every evening and in September, the Lady gave birth to another son, Henry, that Charles acknowledged as his own. Catherine had still not conceived although rumours at various times had suggested she was pregnant. When she fell ill in October, some also said it was due to a miscarriage but given that she was taking the waters for infertility in July and September, it seems hardly likely. It was just wishful thinking on behalf of the court watchers that knew it was tantamount for the king to have a legitimate heir.

On 17th October, Pepys thought Catherine might be dead and reports in his diary over the next few days on her progress after finding out she was actually suffering from a deliriously high fever. On 20th October, he was told that she was 'as full as the spots of a leopard'[39] with the spotted fever – a general term given to any illness with blemishes so perhaps actually chickenpox or measles. Catherine was so ill that she was even given her last rites and her ladies feared she would soon slip away from them. Charles was distraught, and by her bedside every day where she managed to tell him 'she willingly left all the world but him'.[40] Charles urged her to stay alive, tears streaming down his face, in genuine grief for the queen he had barely come to know. Catherine had her head shaved so that a cap of sacred relics could be placed on her head whilst Charles turned grey with worry. Remedies of the day were tried to improve her health including the placing of dead pigeons on her feet. As the fever took her wits, Catherine fell in and out of consciousness but in her lucid moments she asked that her body be sent to Portugal for burial and that Charles would continue to give her country of birth his protection.

At other times she talked of children, something so important to her. On one occasion she thought she had given birth to a son but that he was ugly and Charles had to reassure her that their imaginary child was pretty. Another time she thought she had three children and that her daughter looked just like her father. When her physician woke her to take a tonic the next morning she asked how the children were. It was all her delirious mind could think of.

Against the odds and some people's wishes, Catherine slowly began to recover, thwarting the gossips of the speculation on who would become the next queen. Charles may have been with her during the day throughout her illness but he had spent every evening with Lady Castlemaine and was still chasing Frances Stuart. Catherine was not ready to leave the king to his mistresses even though at the end of October Pepys recorded that she 'yet talks idle still'.[41] By November, Charles was writing to his sister Minette 'my wife is now out of all danger, though very weake, and it was a very strange feaver, for she talked idly fouer or five dayes after the feaver had left her, but now that is likewise past, and desires me to make her compliments to you and Monsieur, which she will do herself as soone as she gets strength'.[42]

Catherine had to be well enough to meet with a special envoy from France and the French ambassador who carried messages from King Louis XIV for her personal attention. They were admitted to her sparsely decorated bedchamber, adorned with 'pretty pious pictures, and books of devotion; and her holy water at her head as she sleeps, with her clock by her bed-side, wherein a lamp burns that tells her the time of the night at any time'[43] and conversed with her in the 'ruelle' – the space between the bed and the wall. Charles had to help Catherine hear their conversation by repeating it all in her ear as she was experiencing deafness after her fever. The French ambassador was still concerned with her health reporting to King Louis 'They make us hope she is out of danger, but she wanders frequently still, which shows that the brain is affected, for the fever is scarcely high enough to cause that symptom'.[44]

By the 7th November, however, Catherine was strong enough to go to chapel and although her birthday celebrations were more subdued this year, the poet Waller wrote Catherine a poem for her birthday marking how tea had become far more fashionable due to the queen.

Venus her myrtle, Phoebus has her bays;
Tea both excels, which she vouchsafes to praise.
The best of Queens, and best of herbs, we owe
To that bold nation, which the way did show
To the fair region where the sun doth rise,
Whose rich productions we so justly prize.
The Muse's friend, tea does our fancy aid,
Repress those vapors which the head invade,
And keep the palace of the soul serene,
Fit on her birthday to salute the Queen.[45]

In December, Charles was writing to Minette again. 'My wife is now so well, as in a few dayes, she will thanke you herselfe for the consernement you had for her, in her sicknesse. Yesterday, we had a little ball in the privy chamber, where she looked on … Pray send me some images, to put in prayer books. They are for my wife, who can get none here. I assure you it will be a greate present to her…'.[46]

The danger had passed and Charles relieved and grateful that his queen had survived nevertheless could now turn his attention more fully to his chief mistress. Charles' relationship with Lady Castlemaine was not as fervent as it had been. Pepys had even mentioned she had decayed somewhat but the king still enjoyed her company, enough to make her pregnant again by the end of the year. After all the drama of Catherine's illness, the Lady added one of her own by now announcing that she was a Catholic. Her family were horrified and asked Charles to intervene to which he replied 'as for the souls of ladies, he never meddled with that'.[47] Catherine more wryly commented that Lady Castlemaine did not turn to the Catholic faith 'for conscience sake'.[48]

Catherine was well recovered in the new year of 1664 but it was not a happy start. Charles was now focusing his attentions on Frances Stuart 'to the open slighting of the Queene…he values not who sees him or stands by him while he dallies with her openly; and then privately in her chamber below, where the very sentrys observe his going in and out'.[49] Frances was encouraging the king; it would be hard to say no to your sovereign but she also had no intention of becoming his mistress. A game of flirtation would be played out over the coming months. While Frances revelled in his attention, she also kept him at arm's length, sharing stolen kisses but nothing more. It infuriated Lady Castlemaine who had favoured Frances and encouraged the king's relationship with her, but now it drove her to distraction as she felt her power slipping away.

The Count de Grammont made a present of a 'calash' – a glazed coach – to the king in the spring. This was a novelty to behold and all the ladies wanted the chance to be the first to be seen taking a ride in it. Catherine of course should have precedence as queen and took her turn with the Duchess of York but Charles was hounded by both Lady Castlemaine and Frances for which of them would be next. The Lady got to Charles first, begging he take her out but continued by denigrating Frances to the point that when Frances then asked for her turn in the calash, the king acquiesced. Lady Castlemaine was furious and it ended any friendship between herself and the now most popular

Frances.

It was rumoured that Catherine hesitated before going into her own rooms for fear of seeing Frances with the king. It was one thing to know he was smitten and another to have your faced rubbed in it. But Catherine did have a soft spot for Frances who as a Catholic attended mass with her in her private chapel and had prayed over her while she was sick. It was hard not to like the endearing, childlike young woman and after their Sunday service, they often walked together in the park.

Catherine also had a soft spot for her Master of Horse, Edward Montague, and had formed a friendly attachment to him that became the talk of the court. Charles' cronies told the king that Montague's behaviour was inappropriate, he had touched the queen's hand and all knew he was in love with her. Charles summarily dismissed him and Catherine refused to take another Master of Horse whilst he still lived. Catherine would not have jeopardised her position by having an affair nor would her religion have allowed it, but she was loyal and Montague had been a friend amongst the thorns of court. Charles could hardly blame her for finding comfort in a friend when he constantly sought comfort elsewhere.

Life for Catherine did not always miserably revolve around the king and his mistresses. She began to take an active interest in the country's affairs rather than just the king's. Back in March she had attended the opening of parliament with Charles and now began to share his interest in all things nautical. The relationship between England and Holland was once more becoming strained. The first Anglo-Dutch war had been fought between 1652–1654 and after much new shipbuilding England was preparing its fleet for the possibility of more hostilities.

Lord Sandwich, admiral of the fleet, was ordered to put to sea early in July and Catherine did not want to miss it. The king wrote to him 'My wife is so afraid that she shall not see the fleet before it goes out, that she intends to set out from this place

(Whitehall) on Monday next, with the afternoon tide; therefore, let all the yachts, except that which the French ambassador has, be ready at Gravesend by that time'.[50] The Queen-Dowager, Henrietta Maria, accompanied Catherine and Charles to Gravesend and then on to Chatham to inspect the fleet and were back again two days later to check on their progress.

It was a long hot summer made slightly more bearable by the use of shading fans made fashionable by the queen. The fashion was for a pale face and these fans not only helped to cool but kept the sun off the face. Catherine had grown up in Portugal where such fans and masks were used frequently but it was a novelty to the ladies at court that was quickly adopted for their walks around the gardens and parks of London. Catherine still liked the traditional black dress of Portugal but she had fast become enamoured with English fashion. Her ladies had known she was on the mend after her previous illness when she had insisted on a new dress and that summer Catherine and her ladies all wore silver lace gowns, their fans coquettishly held in front of their faces as they walked around St James Park.

Catherine, Frances and Lady Castlemaine all sat for Huysmans, the Flemish portrait painter in those sweltering hot days. Catherine had two portraits painted; one depicting her as a shepherdess and another as St Catherine. Frances wore a soldier's doublet for her portrait. Lady Castlemaine's ignored her swelling stomach. She was pregnant again and gave birth to a daughter, Charlotte in September, who was acknowledged by the king. Days later she was attacked and verbally abused by three men as she returned from an evening at the Duchess of York's. Her maid helped her back to the palace where the king was informed. He immediately had the palace gates closed and arrests were made to try and find the culprits to no avail. The Lady knew she had enemies but was extremely frightened by such a bold attack and Charles spent the evening consoling her.

Catherine also had an uncomfortable experience although

nowhere near as frightening as Lady Castlemaine's. For Catherine, it was a matter of her honour and Portugal's. A new Spanish ambassador, Patricio Omeledio, requested an audience with the queen. She had no wish to meet the man who represented her country of birth's greatest enemy but courtesy dictated she must. Catherine 'being discomposed a little more than could have been wished, and forbidding him in his harangue to speak to her in Spanish, he submitted to her pleasure herein, and continued it in French, acquitting himself therein with all fitting respect on his part'.[51] She had almost caused a diplomatic incident. It was the right of the ambassador to speak his native tongue but Catherine, in her stubbornness, didn't want to hear it.

Catherine was feeling more sure of herself and her position. In October, she accompanied the king to a ship launch at Woolwich but Catherine wanted to take the state barge and sail up river whilst Charles and the Duke of York went by land. After a celebratory lunch, Charles and his men sailed on the Nore, where the Thames meets the North Sea, whilst Catherine turned back for Whitehall but the weather turned nasty, the waves rolling the barge and Catherine's ladies became sick and soaked to the skin. She ordered to put back in to Woolwich and hustled the drenched ladies into the king's waiting coaches leaving Charles to find another way back to London. Rather than being angry, Charles was merely amused.

Their relationship had become a friendly, pleasurable one. It had taken time but they had found areas of mutual interest. Catherine was the only one to pay attention to the king's scientific pastimes and she joined him in the winter to look at the stars and more importantly, to catch sight of a comet lighting up London as it trailed across the sky. The physicist and philosopher Sir Isaac Newton observed the comet throughout December and January. Whilst for some it was an astronomical phenomenon, for others it was a portent of the tragedy times to come.

Chapter Three

War, Plague and Fire
1665–1666

On 4th March 1665, King Charles II officially declared war on the Netherlands. It was the second bout of Anglo-Dutch hostilities, the first having occurred during the Interregnum, before Charles was restored to the throne. Several skirmishes had occurred the previous year, with English privateers commandeering Dutch ships and English soldiers capturing the Dutch colonies of New Netherland and New Amsterdam in North America.

In June, the Battle of Lowestoft was fought and won off the coast of Suffolk. The Duke of York, Lord High Admiral, commanded the English navy to its victory with resounding gunfire that could be heard in London. 'All this day by all people upon the River, and almost everywhere else hereabout were heard the guns, our two fleets for certain being engaged'.[1]

But whilst victory was found for a time at sea, there was to be a devastating defeat of the English people on land. England was no stranger to outbreaks of the plague but this year was to be the most tragic. Although not understood then, the disease was spread by the fleas of infected black rats who had arrived in the London docklands on cargo ships from Amsterdam. In 1664, 24,000 people died of the plague in the Dutch capital alone.

Whilst in London there had been occasional cases of the disease over the winter months, the long hot summer that followed fed the contagion. Streets lined with filth and ordure were breeding grounds for rats who spread across the city taking their infection with them. It ran rife through poor families packed tightly in squalid living conditions but no one was spared the coming onslaught. In a bid to stop the plague spreading, the theatres closed and gatherings of people were banned. It was ordered that dogs and cats be killed to stop the spread (although they weren't to blame) to the tune of 40,000 dogs and 200,000 cats being culled during that summer. Affected houses were daubed with an ominous red cross and only 'nurses' were allowed in and out of the houses for a forty day period. The inhabitants were left to either recover or die.

At the end of June the bill of mortality – a weekly record – reported an increase in plague deaths in the city. Pepys wrote 'The towne grows very sickly, and people to be afeard of it; there dying this last week of the plague 112, from 43 the week before'.[2] It was time for the court to leave London and escape the risk. The Queen-Dowager, Henrietta Maria, left first. Her health had not been good of late. She was suffering from chest problems and asked her son's permission to return to France and take the waters at Bourbon. Charles and Catherine accompanied her as far as the Nore and returned to Whitehall to ready themselves for their own departure.

At first they travelled to Hampton Court but after several servants were affected with the plague whilst there it was decided the king and queen would continue on to Salisbury and the Duke and Duchess of York would head north to York. With them went many of the nobility. Charles left the Duke of Albemarle in charge of the city and the Archbishop of Canterbury remained to give services of comfort. Not everyone left. Pepys stayed on, and the diarist Evelyn, but many others that could fled for their lives. It was estimated that 30,000 people escaped the city and its sickness that summer. Those that couldn't leave tried to stay away from affected areas by camping out in parks or moving further afield to places such as Hampstead Heath. London turned into a ghost town. Gone was the hustle and bustle of daily living. Those that met each other on the street kept their distance, grass grew in the roads and carts for collecting the dead continued their rounds night and soon by day, taking the deceased to be buried in mass burial pits.

Even though most of Catherine's household had been sent back to Portugal, her priests had remained and they and their families all travelled with her when she left the city – enough to fill eight coaches. They stopped first at Farnham where Charles left Catherine to continue her laborious journey on to Wiltshire whilst he went to check on the fortifications in Portsmouth and the Isle of Wight. The plague may have struck his country but they were still at war with the Dutch and ships and defences needed inspecting. Funds would also be needed and Catherine had generously told Charles that her allowance could be used to fund the war preparations.

The queen received a warm welcome at Salisbury where the Mayor presented her with two silver flagons. Her ladies were settled into lodgings around the town but she kept Frances with her in the royal apartments. Although the plague was an ever present threat, strangers were not allowed into Salisbury and the city was on effective lockdown to prevent the disease running through its streets. Catherine found Salisbury quite pleasant. The French ambassador reported that she enjoyed hunting every day after dinner and playing bowls. But her days were saddened by hearing the news that her previous Master of Horse, Edward Montague, had died in a naval battle near Bergen in Norway under the command of the Earl of Sandwich. It was put to her that perhaps now he was gone that the position could be given to his younger brother, Ralph, but Catherine had learnt her lesson when it came to choosing servants. Clarendon could ask the king. She would accede to his wishes. But Charles, wary of another argument, since peace had been so recently obtained, referred the choosing of a new Master of Horse back to Catherine. Neither wanted to make the final decision and so Clarendon, forever the go-between, just employed the man.

Life in Salisbury didn't suit Charles. He was ill for several days in September which alarmed Catherine somewhat. The latest figures for plague deaths in London had peaked at over

7,000 and there was no sign of the plague abating. Thankfully the king's illness wasn't severe. Charles wrote to his sister 'I have been troubled these few dayes past with a collique but I thank God I am now perfectly well againe…I am goeing to make a little turne into dorset sheere for 8 or 9 days to passe away the time till I go to Oxford, believing that this place was the cause of my indisposition'.[3]

The king improved with his time away from the canals and waterways of Salisbury that he blamed for his illness and duly opened parliament at Christ Church in Oxford in October seeking support and funds to continue the war. The whole court had moved with him and Catherine was lodged in Merton College, founded in 1264 by the Bishop of Rochester, with her ladies whilst Charles' carried out state business. Catherine was delighted to find out that she was pregnant that winter – the first pregnancy we have for her that can truly be confirmed. The only sour note was Lady Castlemaine was also pregnant again and gave birth to a son, George, in December whom Charles duly acknowledged. Still Catherine was safe in her own knowledge that the child she carried would be the king's legitimate heir and not just another bastard. She was still determined to outshine Lady Castlemaine in really the only way left to her. Charles was never going to be as smitten with her as he was with his mistress but he showed her respect and devotion. She could return his affection by giving England a much needed legitimate heir.

The plague had run its course with a chill winter killing off the disease and the rats that carried it. Although there were still deaths it was now safe to return to the city. Around 70,000 people and more likely closer to 100,000 people had died. Charles was anxious to return. He wrote to Minette 'I have left my wife at Oxford, but hope that in a fortnight or three weeks to send for her to London where already the Plague is in effect nothing. But our women are afraide of the name of Plague, so that they must have a little time to fancy all cleere'.[4]

After he left, Catherine was anxious to return to Whitehall to be with the king and started to make arrangements to leave for Hampton Court but, to her utter dismay, she lost her much longed for baby. On the 5th February, her physician confirmed her miscarriage but reported that 'the evidence of fecundity must allay the trouble of this loss'.[5] Small comfort for the despairing queen.

However, Catherine was back in London by the second week in February when Pepys went 'down to White Hall, and there saw the Queene at cards with many ladies, but none of our beauties were there. But glad I was to see the Queene so well, who looks prettily; and methinks hath more life than before, since it is confessed of all that she miscarried lately'.[6] Catherine did not have time to shut herself away in grief and needed to take her place back at court and Charles' side.

But the tragedies in Catherine's life had not yet finished. In Portugal, her mother was ill and died in Lisbon on 27th February but the news didn't reach England until the end of March and it was several days before Catherine was told. Pepys knew and recorded that the queen 'being in a course of physick, that they dare not tell it her'.[7] By 21st April, Catherine was aware of what had happened and the court was in mourning with its ladies ordered to wear black, keep their hair plain and uncurled, and their faces unadorned with the stick-on patches that were becoming so popular. Our famous diarist was sorry to see Lady Castlemaine looking so rough without these extra adornments. 'I find her to be a much more ordinary woman than ever I durst have thought she was; and indeed, is not so pretty as Mrs Stewart'.[8]

The king was also suffering with a cold and Catherine remonstrated with Lady Castlemaine that his late nights at her house was making him ill. Cheekily, the Lady retorted that he must be staying somewhere else as he always left her house early. Charles was listening to this exchange and immediately chastised his mistress for speaking to the queen disrespectfully, banishing her from court. The Lady was furious, raging at Charles that if he sent her away, she would have his private letters printed for all to see. Yet within days the king and his mistress were reconciled again. If Charles felt for his queen, it was only for a brief moment before his mistress had him ensnared again.

And the Anglo-Dutch war was continuing. At the beginning of June, a ferocious four-day naval battle took place. The fifty-six ship strong English fleet, under the command of George Monck, Duke of Albemarle, was outnumbered by the eighty-four strong Dutch fleet and its superior guns. Thousands of English men lost their lives. Eight ships were sunk with nine more captured. It was a devastating defeat and after so many losses from the plague, England was once again mourning for its men and boys, those lost at sea and the many more who returned wounded or were taken prisoner. England gained a small victory against the Dutch at another skirmish on St James Day where only 300 English men were lost to the Dutch's reported 5,000 but Charles' funds were running out. He had lost ships, was having to repair more and the sailors hadn't even been paid. War was a costly business and the country could not afford to lose more men's lives.

Catherine spent the long, dry summer in Tunbridge Wells. Her physician recommended another round of daily doses of the waters plus plenty of dancing! A frivolous pastime given the circumstances but one that was felt necessary for the procreation of an heir. A contemporary wrote:

The company are all accommodated with lodgings in little clean convenient habitations, that lie scattered from each other a mile and a half round the wells, where the company meet in the morning. This place consists of a long walk shaded by spreading trees, under which they walk while they are drinking the waters. On one side of this walk is a long row of shops, plentifully stocked with toys and ornamental goods, where there is raffling. On the other side is the market. As soon as the evening comes, every one quits his or her little palace, to assemble on the bowling green, where, in the open air, those who choose dance on a turf more soft and smooth than the finest carpet in the world.[9]

An idyllic English summer spent in the countryside, and one that Catherine hoped would provide a cure and a longed for baby. Charles spent time with her at the waters although since Frances Stuart was also there, he was more likely following his infatuation and Catherine unwittingly sparked further attractions for Charles. Fearing the king may be bored, Catherine asked for some theatrical players to come out from the city for their entertainment and in the troupe came Nell Gwyn and Moll Davis, actresses who would later become his mistresses. It seemed like she would forever be surrounded by Charles' other women.

Not long after the court returned to Whitehall, and it was here in the early hours of 2nd September, that cries of 'Fire! Fire!' rang out in the city. Although it was alarming, it wasn't unusual for this cry to go up in a city of wooden houses. The fire started at a bake house in Pudding Lane, close to London Bridge (although recent historical investigation has placed it more likely 60ft east of Pudding Lane in what is now Monument Street). On being called out to assess the risk, the Lord Mayor, Sir Thomas Bloodworth, declared that 'a woman might piss it out'.[10] But fanned by an easterly wind, it swiftly grew out of control, fed by the tar, pitch, timber and oakum that was stored in adjoining warehouses. By the time the sun rose, London Bridge was aflame and only a gap between buildings acting as a firebreak stopped it from spreading to the south.

Instead it rapidly spread eastwards through the city, taking people by surprise at how quickly it consumed the houses around them. Hastily hiding their valuables in cellars or burying them in their gardens and carrying what they could, the city folk, as they had done with the plague just a year before, fled for their lives.

> *All the sky was of a fiery aspect, like the top of a burning oven, and the light seen for above forty miles round for many nights. God grant that mine eyes may never behold the like, who now saw above 10,000 houses all in one flame. The noise, and cracking, and thunder, of the impetuous flames, the shrieking of the women and children, the hurry of the people, the fall of towers, houses, and churches, was like a hideous storm, and the air all about so hot and inflamed, that, at the last, one was not able to approach it.*[11]

The fire raged for three days, reaching 1700°C at its hottest point. What didn't burn, melted; the chains that closed off city streets, window glass, hinges, bars and church bells. Old St Pauls Cathedral was being used by shop keepers to store their goods in what they hoped was a safe place but its lead roof melted and ran inwards destroying all in its path and gutting the building. Over 10,000 houses, eighty-seven parish churches and major structures like the Royal Exchange and the Custom House were destroyed by the time the wind had died down and firebreaks halted the spread of the destruction. Even more houses and buildings were damaged by the fire and thousands of Londoners were made homeless; makeshift tents and huts becoming their temporary homes. Thankfully loss of life was low.

Plague, war and now fire. These were tragic times and the people looked for someone to blame. It could have been their king but Charles and the Duke of York had been seen fighting the fire themselves, soot smeared and muddy, working with the people to try and save their homes, leather water pails in hand. Clarendon wrote that the royal brothers 'put themselves in great dangers among the burning and falling houses, to give advice and direction what was to be done, underwent as much fatigue as the meanest, and had as little sleep or rest'.[12]

Rumours began that the fire was either set by the Dutch or the French as a precursor to invading the city. To quell the fears of his people, Charles rode to one of the homeless camps at Moorfields and told them there was no plot, the fire was just an act of God and that he would take care of his Londoners. Guards were sent to distribute coal, bread and barely edible navy biscuits to the needy as a start but Charles had grander plans now for the rebuilding of his city.

Catherine had waited anxiously at Whitehall for news every day, spending hours in her chapel praying for the city's deliverance and the safety of her husband. The fire had died out before it reached Whitehall but still the king had ordered many of their valuables to be sent to Hampton Court and now she need to organise their return. Charles as well was discussing with her his plans of renewing the city. It had long been his desire that more of London should be built in stone rather than wood. Just eighteen months previously he had written to the Lord Mayor to discuss new building regulations as he feared the risk of fire to an overcrowded, poorly constructed city. Catherine was about to go riding, dressed in a cavalier habit, horseman's coat and hat with impressive feather, when Charles entered her bedchamber with the Duke of York and the diarist Evelyn. Evelyn and Christopher Wren, the renowned architect, had surveyed the damage in London and had now come up with a plan for its renewal which was eagerly discussed. Ideas abounded, but the people didn't wait for the king's instructions and had already begun to cobble their homes back together. Charles ordered that any new building be made of brick or stone but the reality was people made do with what they could find, eager to restart their lives and livelihoods.

Lady Castlemaine was as eager to keep her livelihood going – as mistress to the king. It had long been rumoured that much of Charles' funds ended up paying off her gambling debts or was used to buy her expensive gifts, jewellery and furniture. While many in London were rebuilding their houses, the Office of Works started a major refurbishment of Barbara's rooms at Whitehall, even though some had said she was far out of favour. The new oratory, bathroom, library 'with seven-foot-high, glass-fronted bookcases, a grand staircase to the privy...and even an aviary'[13] showed otherwise.

All this cost vast amounts of money. To try to increase the funds in England's coffers, Charles instructed Sir Robert Southwell, the English ambassador at Lisbon, to step up his efforts to obtain the rest of Catherine's dowry. He reminded King Alphonso, the queen's brother, that Donna Luiza had promised the rest of the dowry would be payed within a year of Catherine's marriage. Southwell insisted 'several years are now elapsed without accomplishment of the latter payment and his Majesty of Great Britain hath for some years past been engaged in a sharpe and expensive war...he hath therefore commanded his said envoy to...demand in his name from Your Majesty the full satisfaction of the said sum in arrears...'.[14] There was also a veiled threat that England would remove its protection from Portugal if the dowry wasn't paid but King Alphonso could not give what he did not have and England became none the richer.

London gradually began to return to normal. The theatres reopened in November, giving some of their profits to the city's 65,000 homeless. Rebuilding of homes would long continue. Many still lived in temporary accommodation, some moved in with relatives, others left the city to live in other towns or emigrated to the colonies for a fresh start. Shopkeepers who had plied their goods at the Royal Exchange relocated to Gresham College and reopened in December. Others vendors moved to parts of the city that had been unaffected.

After such tumultuous times, Catherine's birthday celebrations gave some sparkle to the end of the year. It relieved the ladies of having to wear mourning black and for this night it was silver and white lace. Pepys had managed to get himself up into a loft space to watch the evening unfold below him.

Anon, the house grew full, and the candles light, and the King and Queene and all the ladies sat; and it was, indeed, a glorious sight to see Mrs. Stewart in black and white lace, and her head and shoulders dressed with diamonds (only the Queen none) and the king in his rich vest of some rich silk, and silver trimming...Presently, after the king was come in, he took the queen, and about fourteen more couple there were, and began the Bransles...After the Bransles, then to a Corant, and now and then a French dance; but that so rare that the Corants grew tiresome, that I wished it done. Only Mrs. Stewart danced mighty finely, and many French dances, specially one the King called the New Dance, which was very pretty; but upon the whole matter, the business of the dancing of itself was not extraordinary pleasing. But the clothes and sight of the persons was indeed very pleasing, and worth my coming, being never likely to see more gallantry while I live, if I should come twenty times.[15]

There was all the hope that the next year would be a far better one.

Chapter Four

Mistresses and Enemies
1667–1669

1667 did not start well for Catherine. There were factions at court who were not happy that the succession was still open with no heir apparent. Would it not be as well for Charles to put aside his Portuguese queen and marry a more fecund bride? Many thought so and sought ways to rid Charles of his queen. The Earl of Bristol sent two friars to Portugal to collect evidence to prove it had been known that Catherine couldn't have children before her marriage but of course nobody had evidence – who could have such proof? Least of all Catherine herself who prayed every day for an heir and took all the remedies and treatments her physicians recommended. Charles refused to believe Catherine had known she was barren, although it was rumoured he had asked the Archbishop of Canterbury whether a divorce could be possible.

Charles knew what Catherine went through to boost her fertility and he never swayed in his loyalty to her as his queen. Romantically, he had other ideas and was happily chasing Frances Stuart – an entertaining plaything – not a replacement for his wife. Lady Castlemaine and the queen were far from his mind as he stole kisses from Frances in the corridors and chased her through the galleries of Whitehall. Yet Frances would not let him do more than that and it drove him mad. This young girl resisting her king was a novelty and an annoyance but it was part of the chase. He pursued her relentlessly as she continued to encourage him.

And while Charles was otherwise engaged, the nobles surrounding him looked to blame someone for the lack of a legitimate heir. The man who bore the brunt of the courtier's dissatisfaction with their queen was the Lord Chancellor, Clarendon. Never popular, they now blamed him for the Portuguese marriage with always the whisper that he had known Catherine was barren and only sought to further his own family's rise with his daughter's marriage to the Duke of York. His son, Henry Hyde, had also recently been made Catherine's Lord Chamberlain, adding fuel to the fire.

It was not just the nobles at court who were blaming Clarendon. The people too disliked the king's chancellor. Someone wittily daubed the words *Three sights to be seen, Dunkirk, Tangiers and a barren queen* outside his house. And a ditty did the rounds of court:

God bless Queen Kate
Our sovereign's mate,
Of the royal house of Lisbon.
But the devil take Hyde,
And the bishop beside,
Who made her bone of his bone.[1]

Clarendon had been instrumental in selling Dunkirk to France for £400,000 but ultimately he had only been doing his king's bidding. The occupation of Tangier was a drain on England's treasury and perhaps should have been sold off and he was blamed for that too. His downfall was imminent but Charles was not yet ready to see his chancellor be replaced, or was too distracted to make the change.

Frances was a pleasant diversion. All could see it and Lady Castlemaine, with vengeance in mind, took her chance to stir the pot. If there had been any friendship left between Frances and Barbara it would truly be gone now. The Lady told Charles that if he visited Frances' chamber that night, he would find out the true depth of her devotion. Intrigued, the king strode into Frances' chamber, to find the Duke of Richmond sitting on Frances' pillow, whispering sweet nothings in her ear, as she reclined in bed. Seeing the king, the duke immediately leapt up and out of the window, making his escape while Charles ranted at the woman he had hoped to bed. Frances was indignant. She had her virtue to protect. Why could she not entertain a man who had honest intentions towards her? She longed for marriage, a home, stability. It had been fun flirting with the king but she wanted now what he could not give. What he could never give. Stung by her words, Charles stormed through the palace of Whitehall, back to his chamber.

Knowing the king was furious with her, Frances flung herself on the mercy of the queen, begging Catherine to forgive her if she had ever caused her pain by encouraging Charles' attentions. She asked for her protection and through her tears, Frances sobbed out that she would even join a convent if it pleased their majesties. Anything but to be away from court and the pain she had caused. Catherine wiped the tears away and promised to help her.

The queen remonstrated with Charles. Frances was a young girl who deserved a good marriage. She was from a noble family and Charles should see that the duke was a suitable match for her. Charles had banished the man from court but he craftily agreed. They could marry all right but only if the duke proved he was worthy and of sufficient wealth. If he showed Charles details of his financial situation and they were deemed satisfactory, then he may have his bride. Out of Catherine's earshot, he informed Clarendon to look into all the duke's dealings and find something amiss, something on which he could refuse the marriage.

Pepys definitely thought that the marriage would go ahead. On 19th March, he wrote 'the match is concluded between the Duke of Richmond and Mrs. Stewart, which I am well enough pleased with; and it is pretty to consider how his quality will allay people's talk; whereas, had a meaner person married her, he would for certain have been reckoned a cuckold at first-dash'.[2]

Clarendon was having trouble finding out anything negative about the duke. Taking matters into her own hands, Frances refused to wait for permission any longer. At the end of March, she wrapped herself warmly against the stormy night and left Whitehall making her way across London Bridge. At The Bear at the Bridge Foot, a tavern on the southern side of the river, the duke was waiting with a carriage to take her to his ancestral home of Cobham Hall where they were married at the beginning of April. Charles vowed he would never allow her or her husband into his presence ever again. He was heartbroken and wretched, taking it out on everyone around him and the pain didn't subside. Charles was still missing Frances later in the year when he told Minette:

> ...how hard a thing tis to swallow an injury done by a person I had so much tendernesse for, you will in some degree excuse the resentment I use towards her; you know my good nature enough to believe that I could not be so severe, if I had not great provocation, and I assure you her carriage towards me has been as bad as breach of frindship and faith can make it, therefore I hope you will pardon me if I cannot so soon forget an injury which went so neere my hart.[3]

But there were always other entertainments to distract him as he pondered on his loss of Frances. He could watch Nell and Moll, his fine young actresses, at the theatres occasionally accompanied by Catherine. It wasn't a comfortable experience for the queen knowing that the king was watching his lovers. And there was no respect for her there either. On one occasion, she sat waiting for the performance to start which seemed to be delayed. She sent a message for the play to commence immediately to which the leading man, Cardell Goodman, retorted 'I care not if the playhouse be filled with queens from top to bottom. I will not tread the stage until my duchess comes'[4] referring to Lady

Castlemaine, her patronage of the theatre and her amours with its players making her their favourite.

There was a great masked ball held in April when the king and queen danced together in public. For St George's day, Charles headed the ceremonies for the knights of the Order of the Garter. After the church service, a sumptuous banquet was held. Charles sat alone on an elevated throne at the head of the room with his knights sitting at tables stretched out before him. 'About the middle of the dinner, the Knights drank the King's health, then the King, theirs, when the trumpets and music played and sounded, the guns going off at the Tower'.[5] Catherine came in to stand by the king for a while but left when a food fight started. There were forty different dishes so the knights had ample ammunition. Evelyn wrote that 'the cheer was extraordinary' but 'stayed no longer than this sport began, for fear of disorder'.[6] It sounds like the feast was getting a little out of hand!

The knights may have had one uproarious evening but the king's trouble with women was not yet over. Catherine must have seemed like the calm in the storm his mistresses created around him. On hearing that the Duke of Buckingham had been imprisoned for misconduct, Lady Castlemaine raged at Charles and scolded him for such an act. The lady and the duke were close – definitely cousins, possibly lovers. Buckingham was the son of George Villiers, King James I's favourite and rumoured lover who had been assassinated in 1628. Like his father, he was a consummate courtier, one of Charles' 'merry men' who liked nothing better than to fill his days with wine and women. Charles had made him a Gentleman of his Bedchamber and he sat on the Privy Council but he was constantly misbehaving and Charles had seen fit to have him punished this time.

Lady Castlemaine's fury was intense and she railed at the king for his own transgression. Charles argued back calling her a jade and telling her not to meddle in things that did not concern her. With no curb on her tongue, Lady Castlemaine called her king a fool and 'that if he were not a fool, he would not suffer his business to be carried on by fools that did not understand them, and cause his best subjects, and those best able to serve him, to be imprisoned'.[7] Charles amazingly gave in and released the duke. Something that would not bode well for Catherine. Buckingham had no love for the queen and wanted her gone.

There was no respite for Charles. He had hoped to find it in the arms of Nell Gwyn but she had run away with Lord Buckhurst, one of Charles' gentlemen of the bedchamber, although he would abandon her before too long. Moll Davis was a comfort to him but a thorn in Catherine's side. She danced so seductively in front of the queen when called to perform before Charles that Catherine had to leave the room. Yet again Charles' philandering was being rubbed in her face and she didn't need to see it even though she was well aware of what was going on. Other actresses were led up the back stairs to see the king from time to time by William Chiffinch, Keeper of the King's Closet and Pictures, including Elizabeth Farley and Beck Marshall. Apart from Charles, Chiffinch was the only one to have a key to the king's closet, not even Catherine could enter this space unless permitted entrance.

Peace talks with the Dutch had begun earlier in the year but were drawn out by indecision and negotiation. The English fleet had been laid up and neglected during the times of plague and fire and there was little money to continue the war or refit the ships. The Dutch took their chance to deal a final blow. In June, their fleet arrived off the coast of Kent. They took the fort at Sheerness and sailed on up the Medway to burst through the chain protecting the entrance to Chatham boatyard. Charles' flagship the *Royal Charles* was captured as well as the *Unity* and the *Royal Oak*, *Royal James* and *Loyal London* plus ten smaller ships were burnt in the water. People feared a Dutch invasion but the fleet withdrew after the damage was done, taking with it the *Royal*

Charles as a final humiliating act. People lambasted the king for being slow to rally England's defences and also because it was rumoured he had sat out the whole ordeal at Lady Castlemaine's with others who were 'all mad in hunting of a poor moth'.[8] For a king who had lost his own father to the people's will, his attitude was careless. However, on 21st July, the treaty of Breda was signed, signalling the end of the second Anglo-Dutch war and for a time peace in England.

But there was no peace for the Lord Chancellor. Someone had to take the blame for the disaster at Chatham and Clarendon's enemies who had been working towards his downfall saw their opportunity. Even though Clarendon had been against the Dutch war, they convinced Charles to dismiss him. It was a further blow for the aging chancellor who was forced to give up his seal of office. His wife and grandsons had died in the summer, his house attacked and windows broken.

Still he defended his corner until October when Charles agreed that Clarendon could be impeached on seventeen charges. When the issue was brought before the House of Lords, Clarendon's peers refused to accept the accusations against him. With rumours that Charles would convene a court and trial headed by Buckingham – a case that would result in the chancellor's execution – Clarendon fled to France.

With Clarendon gone, the Duke of Buckingham rose in power. He was part of the 'CABAL' made up of Clifford, Arlington, Buckingham, Ashley, and Lauderdale that now advised the king. They were no supporters of Catherine and Buckingham now took his chance to push Charles to get rid of his barren queen.

Buckingham came up with the astonishing idea of kidnapping Catherine and having her transported to a plantation in America. No harm would come to her and she could live out her life there giving Charles grounds for divorce based on her desertion. Charles thankfully was appalled at the suggestion and told Buckingham that 'it would be a wicked thing to make a poor woman miserable only because she is my wife, and has no children by me, which is no fault of hers'.[9] Trying another tack, Buckingham then put forward the idea that Catherine be sent to a convent. Charles was more amenable to Catherine taking her vows and living the religious life – but only if she wanted to. He knew how devout she was and although he still hoped that Catherine would bear him an heir, if this was her wish he would grant it. For a moment, the Buckingham faction thought they had found a way to get rid of the queen until she firmly announced 'she had no vocation for the religious life'.[10]

Regardless of those that plotted against her, Catherine continued to live at court and even embraced a more frivolous side to it. There were times when Catherine grew tired of being the pious, pitied wife and she joined in the merriment and playfulness of the court with her ladies. They often went out in the evening in sedan chairs to attend masquerades, balls and dances. One night Catherine joined them but got split up from her party and unceremoniously was left in the street when her sedan bearer went off for a beer! The queen had to gather up her skirts and increasingly anxious, find another chair to take her back to Whitehall. If her enemies had been watching it would have been the ideal time to kidnap her but she made it safely back to Whitehall, albeit shaken and frightened by her night on the town.

It seems that whether Catherine joined in the fun or remained to one side, she was still damned if she did and damned if she didn't. Andrew Marvell wrote a scathing and hurtful poem around this time.

Reform great Queen the errors of your youth
And hear a thing you never heard, called truth;
Poor private balls content the fairy Queen,
She must dance (and dance abominably) to be seen.

Ill-natured little goblin, and designed
For nothing but to dance and vex mankind.
What wiser thing could our great monarch do
Than root ambition out, by showing you?
You can the most aspiring thoughts pull down,
For who would have his wife, to have his crown?
What will be next, unless you please to go
And dance among your fellow fiends below?
There as upon the Stygian lake you float,
You may o'erset and sink the laden boat;
While we the funeral rites devoutly pay,
And dance for joy, that you are dance away.[11]

No matter who wanted to get rid of her, Catherine was determined to stay and determined to dance. She showed them all at
a ball held for her birthday, joining in with the dances she had
painstakingly learnt until she was exhausted. And early the
following year she really put the plotters out by falling pregnant.
Now there could definitely be no plans to remove her while she
carried the king's child. Comforted by her condition, Catherine
ignored Charles' increasing infatuation with his theatrical
mistresses. Both Moll Davis and Nell Gwyn were regular
features in his life now. Both had come from humble
backgrounds but sought to become the country's finest actresses.
Pepys suggested Moll was the illegitimate daughter of Thomas
Howard, the Earl of Berkshire, for all the good it did her, whilst
Nell was reared by a drunken mother and started her career in
the theatre as an orange girl, selling small, sweet china oranges
to the audience for sixpence a piece.

Nell didn't take to rivals kindly especially one's of her own
ilk. The king's ladies she couldn't contend with but she was
determined to best Moll. One day on hearing that her rival was
to dine privately with the king, Nell invited her to afternoon tea.
Under the pretext of a cordial tête-à-tête, Nell had arranged for a

strong laxative to be slipped into Moll's sweetmeats. The poor girl had a very unpleasant evening with the king and Nell was delighted!

Catherine had no time for such frivolities and was distracted by the changes that were happening in Portugal. Her eldest brother King Alphonso had been deposed by her younger brother Pedro. Sad, mad Alphonso had tried so hard to rule but a Council of State intervened in his ever increasing insanity and sent him to the Azores and on to Sintra where he was kept a virtual prisoner for the rest of his life. He had married in 1666 but the Queen had taken up residence in a convent due to his mistreatment of his wife. Their marriage was annulled on the grounds of non-consummation and Pedro, now Prince Regent, married his brother's wife.

As Portugal settled into a peaceful period, London broke out in dissent. Known as the Bawdy House riots, the brothels and bawdy houses of the East End were looted and destroyed by hundreds of young men unhappy with the king's recent proclamation on private worship and enforcement of the Act of Uniformity. They were sick of double standards and the debauchery and licentiousness of his court. Prostitutes were attacked and Lady Castlemaine, who some considered the greatest of them all, was lambasted. A satirical pamphlet, *The Poor Whores Petition*, addressed her as 'the most splendid, illustrious, serene, and eminent lady of pleasure'[12] and called on her to help out her fellow 'sisters'. Another pamphlet written in response, *The Gracious Answer*, added further insult to injury. Charles' flamboyant response and snub was to give Lady Castlemaine the fine residence of Berkshire House and settle on her a pension of £4,700 a year. The dissenters may have made their point but he would not change his policies, his ways or his mistresses for anyone.

And someone who he had missed sorely was back at court.

Frances, now the Duchess of Richmond, had returned to visit Catherine and had taken rooms in Somerset House with her husband but not long after her arrival, she sickened with a severe dose of smallpox. Catherine too had taken to her bed. She lost the baby she was carrying and was once more plunged into a world of sadness and despair.

Although Charles was disappointed he was more concerned with his beloved Frances. His letter to Minette dated 7th May started '…I was at the Duchesse of Richmond's who, you know, I have not seene this twelve monthes, and shee put it out of my heade that it was post day. She is not much marked with the smale pox, and I must confesses this last affliction made me pardon all that is past…'[13] Only later in the letter does he happen to mention 'my wife miscarried this morning, and though I am troubled at it, yet I am glad that 'tis evident she was with childe, which I will not deny you; till now, I did feare she was not capable of. The Physisians do intend to put her into a course of physique, which they are confident will make her holde faster next time'.[14]

Catherine began to mend with more recommendations from her physicians as did Frances although one of her eyes was impaired. Pepys wrote of them, 'The King begins to be mightily reclaimed, and sups every night with great pleasure with the Queen; and yet, it seems, he is mighty hot upon the Duchess of Richmond…he did…go to Somerset House, and there, the garden door not being open, himself clambered over the wall to make a visit to her, which is a horrid shame!'[15]

Frances was probably back to keeping Charles at bay as she was faithful to her queen and husband. Catherine rewarded her with a position as one of her ladies of the bedchamber which came with lodgings at the Bowling Green, Whitehall. Catherine was glad to have her companion back. Someone she could confide in and share her worries. Buckingham was again pressing the king to divorce her and it was a welcome break to head to Tunbridge Wells again to take the waters. She would make the most of the summer yet it was tinged with sadness. 'The Queen even surpassed her usual attentions in inventing and supporting entertainments: she endeavoured to increase the natural ease and freedom of Tunbridge, by dispensing with, rather than requiring, those ceremonies that were due to her presence; and, confining in the bottom of her heart that grief and uneasiness she could not overcome...'.[16]

Catherine patronised a group of Italian singers and at the end of September they delighted her by serenading the queen and her ladies from outside her windows at Whitehall. Pepys went along to hear them. 'So I to White Hall, and there all the evening on the Queen's side; and it being a most summerlike day, and a fine warm evening, the Italians come in a barge under the leads, before the Queen's drawing-room; and so the Queen and ladies went out, and heard them, for almost an hour: and it was indeed very good together; but yet there was but one voice that alone did appear considerable, and that was Seignor Joanni'.[17]

Unknown to many, Catherine also patronised a secret convent in Hammersmith. She had invited the Institute of the Blessed Virgin Mary (Sisters of Loreto), founded by Mary Ward in 1609, to establish a house in London. They were committed to educating young girls but their ideas were ahead of the times and the order had been suppressed in 1631. Hiding their true identities by not wearing habits, they set up a boarding for girls and Catherine continued to fund them throughout the following years.

Both the king and queen went on progress in the autumn to Audley End, Euston and Newmarket and ended the year with the usual festivities for Catherine's birthday and the New Year. Their relationship was now one of mutual understanding and they took pleasure in each other's company. So much so that come the spring, Catherine was expecting again.

Charles hinted of a pregnancy when he wrote to his sister on

6th May 1669. 'My wife has been a little indisposed some few dayes, and there is hopes that it will prove a disease not displeasing to me.' But by the beginning of June he was writing '...my wife, after all our hopes, has miscarried againe, without any visible accident. The physicians are divided whether it were a false conception or a good one...'[18] Catherine may however have experienced a fright that led to the miscarriage. A contemporary letter reported that 'one of the King's tame foxes, which, stealing after the King unknown into the bedchamber, lay there all night, and in the morning, very early, leaped upon the bed, and run over the Queen's face and into the bed'.[19] It was another devastating blow to Catherine.

She had spent the past few years determined to produce an heir, to best Lady Castlemaine, outdo all the king's mistresses and provide the king with a legitimate son. Now she began to realise this might not come to be. Lady Castlemaine had faded into the background as had Moll Davis and now the king's only true mistress was Nell Gwyn. Catherine wasn't threatened by her. Little Nell did nothing to upset her life at court. She had been given the position of Lady of the Queen's Privy Chamber but it was a token role to enable her to draw a salary. Nell had no compunction to hurt and embarrass the queen by attending on her.

That summer Charles told Catherine he had a cold and he would be staying abed. Catherine decided to make sure he was well and visited his chambers early one morning. Seeing the king was not ailing too badly she turned to go and spotted one of Nell's little slippers peeking out from under the bed. 'I will not stay for fear the pretty fool that owns that little slipper might take cold,'[20] she told him. She was resigned to his amours by now. She could be the king's wife, his loyal companion and support, let others be his lovers.

He needed her support in September when his mother, Henrietta Maria, the Queen-Dowager died in Colombes, France.

She had not been well for some time but she had met her illnesses head on as she had done with all the trouble in her life. Feeling unwell, her doctor had convinced her to take a sedative, three grains of laudanum, to help her sleep. She never woke up. Catherine mourned the loss of her mother-in-law as she was laid to rest in the Basilica of Saint-Denis in Paris. The Queen-Dowager had been a supportive and true friend in the early months of her marriage to her son and now Catherine was granted Henrietta Maria's favourite residence, Somerset House. It was a place that would become her refuge and her sanctuary in the coming years.

Chapter Five

A French Alliance
1670–1673

Catherine's enemies had more ammunition in March 1670 when a ground-breaking bill was introduced to Parliament that would allow Lord Roos, a Whig politician, to divorce his wife and remarry. Before now the church could grant a divorce but only parliament had the right to grant remarriage. Charles attended the debate and the Duke of Buckingham took this as a sign that the king was seriously considering divorcing Catherine. He attempted to get his own bill passed – a Royal Divorce and Remarriage Bill – but Charles stopped him. He had no need to remarry. He had a wife and one who was plaint and amenable enough to allow him to live the way he wanted. As far as he was concerned, the queen was happy enough, and his mistresses gave him pleasure. Nell was keeping him warm at night and was expecting his child. In May she gave birth to his son, Charles.

Just days later, the court welcomed a visitor that Charles had been dying to see, his sister, Minette. But this was no ordinary family reunion. Minette had been charged by the king of France to negotiate a secret treaty that would be mutually beneficial between the two countries. It had been a hard battle for Minette to extricate herself from her possessive husband, the Duc d'Orleans, but King Louis XIV knew that Minette would be the best ambassador to convince Charles of the value of such an alliance.

Minette arrived in Dover with an entourage of over 200 people, including five maids of honour. One in particular, Louise de Kérouaille, caught Charles' eye but for now there were negotiations to discuss in private against the backdrop of festivities and banquets in his sister's honour. On 29th May the court relocated to Canterbury and Catherine met her sister-in-law for the first time. Minette thought she was 'a very good woman, not handsome, but so kind and excellent it is impossible not to love her'.[1]

To keep Buckingham occupied, Charles gave him the job of negotiating a formal treaty with France but tucked away with Minette, they formulated a similar Anglo-French alliance against the Dutch but with the secret clause that Charles would openly declare himself a Roman Catholic and bring Catholicism back to England. For this Louis would give him £200,000 and 6,000 French troops to begin with, and £300,000 a year to continue the war with the Dutch. The treaty was signed on 1st June by Colbert de Croissy for France and the Lords Arlington and Arundel, Sir Thomas Clifford and Sir Richard Bellings for England. Bellings was Catherine's man and it would lead us to believe that Catherine was aware of the treaty. It had always been Catherine's wish that Charles joined her in her own faith and she must have been delighted that this was now a possibility, in her eyes at least. For Charles to openly declare himself Catholic could risk civil war, hence the secrecy.

Too soon, it was Minette's time to return to France and Charles was genuinely bereft to see her go. He showered her with gifts and asked that she leave him a jewel of her own. When Louise de Kérouaille was ushered in with a casket from which Charles was to choose a token, he told Minette that here was the jewel he most coveted, the girl herself. His sister looked at him indulgently but refused. Louise must return to France – for now.

Eighteen days after Minette's departure, she was dead, believed poisoned by her husband, although no proof was ever found. The bright and vivacious sister of King Charles had been feeling unwell since her long voyage and settling down after dinner one evening had complained of pains in her side. She slept for a while and waking still in pain asked for a cup of chicory water to aid her indigestion. As she grew worse, it was obvious that she was dying. The French king and queen arrived from Paris with other nobles to comfort her in her final hours. Minette was lucid at times and asked Ralph Montagu, the English ambassador, to give her ring to her brother and ordered a servant to give the ambassador her letters from Charles, sensitive as they were. Montagu tried to ask her if she had been poisoned but a priest interrupted him. She managed to whisper though 'If this is true you must never let the King, my brother, know of it. Spare him the grief at all events and do not let him take revenge on the King here for he is at least not guilty'.[2] Minette would do nothing to jeopardise the secret treaty between the two countries that she loved.

Louis XIV was appalled at Minette's death, especially since poison had been mentioned. For there to be such a scandal now could ruin everything with Charles. A post mortem was ordered and Louis' doctors declared that Minette had died of cholera. The English doctors were not convinced but, given the political situation, signed her death certificate.

Charles certainly believed the rumours, crying out 'Monsieur is a villian!'[3] referring to her husband the duc when he heard the news. But Minette had not wanted the treaty to fail, it was her final gift to her brother and Charles, realising that making any formal accusation would ruin what she had worked so hard to achieve, let it go. He sent Buckingham to France to represent him at Minette's funeral while he stayed at Whitehall to be comforted by Catherine, Nell and even Frances, who had grown up with Minette, and shared in his sorrow.

Buckingham, as crafty as ever, mentioned to King Louis after the funeral that Louise de Kérouaille was now without mistress and might serve both courts well if she were to be given a position at the English court. Ever watchful for a way to bring Catherine down, he saw in Louise a possibility to ensnare the king's affections once and for all. It was agreed that Louise would join the court as one of Catherine's maids of honour and

Buckingham lent her his carriage to take her to Dieppe for her onward journey. Hearing his pregnant mistress was about to give birth, Buckingham sailed quickly back to England, forgetting his charge. Stranded, Louise, who would never forgive Buckingham for such a slight, waited days until Lord Arlington sent a boat and servants to accompany her to Whitehall.

Catherine allowed her into her chambers reluctantly. Louise was an unknown quantity but if Charles' sister had trusted her, perhaps Catherine could too. Louise with her curly dark hair and brown eyes was from a noble but poor Brittany family. She had been educated in an Ursuline convent near Brest before joining Minette's entourage as one of her ladies and had all the grace and manners of the French court, bringing with her new fashions and styles that made her the talk of the town.

Nell disliked her from the start giving her the nicknames of 'weeping willow' and 'squintabella'.[4] Louise was a threat to her position as mistress and her popularity put Nell's nose out if joint. Nell wasn't exactly lacking in admirers though. She had just returned to the stage and was rehearsing her role as Almahide, Queen of the Moors, for Dryden's play *The Conquest of Granada*. Louise wasn't about to jump straight into bed with the king anyway. He was still in mourning for his sister and although Louise was a great comfort to him, sharing with him stories of his sister's life in France, he had not yet begun the chase for her virtue.

Lady Castlemaine wasn't too perturbed by the arrival of Louise. She knew she no longer had the king's highest favours but still he conferred the titles of Duchess of Cleveland, Baroness Nonsuch and Countess of Southampton on her 'in consideration of her noble descent, her father's death in the service of the crown, and by reason of her personal virtues',[5] as well as considerable grants.

With the women around him reasonably happy, Charles was more concerned with his first born son, the Duke of Monmouth.

In December 1670, he had been involved, either personally or through giving orders, in an altercation with Sir John Coventry whose nose was slit to the bone during the incident. It caused an outcry in Parliament causing the 'Coventry Act' to be passed, a bill to prevent malicious maiming and wounding, making such attacks a felony. Monmouth's part in the assault was hushed up but Charles was becoming increasingly concerned with his son's behaviour.

The winter months were caught up in rehearsals for a grand ballet to be held at Whitehall in February 1671 to mark the end of the mourning period for Charles' sister. Catherine, Frances and Louise with the Duchesses of Monmouth and Buckingham led the dances. Seamstresses had been busy designing three costumes for each of the ladies and new music was composed for their pleasure. Crowds had gathered at the palace from as early as 4pm for the evening performance and 'After the ballet was over several others danced, as the Duke of York, and the King, and the Duke of Buckingham. And the Duchess of Cleveland was very fine in a rich petticoat and halfe shirte and a short man's coat very richly laced, a periwig, cravat and hat'.[6]

Nell had not been invited; her position not suitably raised to attend with the other ladies. The Duchess of York was also absent, heavily pregnant at the time and also suffering with breast cancer. After the birth of her daughter Catherine, she fell seriously ill. Catherine stayed by her bedside throughout her final days. Anne had secretly converted to Catholicism and Burnet suggested that the queen had only cared for her to make sure the correct prayers were said. He recorded 'that the bishop intended to administer the sacrament, and read the service for the sick to the Duchess of York, but when he saw the queen sitting by her bedside, his modesty deterred him from reading prayers which would, probably, have driven her majesty out of the room; but, that not being done, she, pretending kindness, would not leave her'.[7] Even when Catherine was altruistic she was slandered.

The Duke of York was also unhappy with her despite her care of his wife. The Coldstream Guards had been appointed as the Queen's Guards and Catherine had believed they would be second in line after the kings. The Duke of York however felt his regiment should have seniority over the queen's guards and made Charles promise this would be so. Catherine with an uncharacteristic display of stubbornness refused to allow this to happen. By rights, her guards should be the second regiment and she would not give in to the duke. James, seeing he wasn't going to win this one, told Charles 'he saw that his majesty was teased by the women and others on that account, and though he must consider it a hardship, he would voluntarily release him from his promise; for, whatever others did, he was resolved never to make him uneasy for any concern of his'.[8] James may have been annoyed with her but when Catherine knew she was right, she stuck to her guns, literally in this case, and she didn't hold it against him. He had just lost his three-year-old son, Edgar too. Knowing his daughters, Mary and Anne, were now motherless, she made sure they were cared for earning her the nickname of 'mother' of the court. It may have pained her to not have her own children but she took great pleasure in being maternal to others.

Life for Catherine was now much quieter. Louise was taking up Charles' time and she had no wish to watch this next flirtation play out. In June she moved to Somerset House and started a new life away from court. The house – now more of a palace – had originally been built for Edward Seymour, Duke of Somerset and Lord Protector in 1551. By the early 1600s it had passed to James I's wife, Anne of Denmark and became known as Denmark House. Anne employed the famous architect Inigo Jones to remodel and renovate much of the building adding a new courtyard and open arcade. By Charles I's reign, Henrietta Maria was in charge of more renovation and redecoration including the building of her Catholic chapel and later a new riverfront gallery.

Now Catherine asked Christopher Wren to redecorate Somerset House to her taste. It was a perfect antidote to Whitehall. She was still very much a fixture at balls and masques and would support Charles when she was needed but she took great pride in managing a household away from the intrigues and machinations of the court nobles.

Catherine's outlook on life greatly improved giving her a sense of freedom and playfulness. Her closest companions were the Duchess of Richmond and the Duchess of Buckingham. Charles Lyttleton, governor of Harwich saw them at Hampton Court in the summer 'when the Queene was at Hampton Court one day rideing abroad, it raining and my Lady Marshall and Lady Gerrard being in her coach, her Majestie came into ye coach and called in the two Duchesses, Buck and Richmond, and left the other ladyes upon ye common to shift for themselves, wch you may believe was no small greife to them'.[9]

During the summer, Catherine went on progress with the king and their first stop was at Audley End, the home of the Earl of Suffolk. The queen thought it might be fun to visit the great annual fair nearby at Saffron Walden with the Duchesses of Buckingham and Richmond but disguised as ordinary women. They dressed themselves in what they thought were rustic clothes, short petticoats and waistcoats, and with three trusty servants they rode to the fair. No sooner had they got there than people started to notice them. Their clothing didn't exactly match the normal peoples and as Catherine asked to buy some yellow stockings for her sweetheart at a stall, her upper class accent was detected. Her chaperone, Sir Bernard Gascoigne, asked for gloves with blue stitching for his sweetheart too and it was obvious to the gathered country folk that these were not ordinary fair-goers. People began to follow the intrepid ladies and when someone pointed out that it was indeed the queen as they had seen her at a state dinner, a crowd gathered around them forcing them to make a dash for their horses and flee back to Audley End, the people of Saffron Walden following them all the way.

The next day the king and queen moved on to Euston Hall, Lord Arlington's residence near Newmarket and from here Charles took a trip to Yarmouth with the Duke of York agreeing to meet up with Catherine at Norwich. On a pouring wet day, Charles and his entourage met the mayor and his aldermen at Trowsebridge who then had to cross the city to meet Catherine who was entering from the other side. The town's people thronged the streets to see the royal couple as they were escorted to Lord Henry Howard's lodgings in King Street for feasting and entertainment and onwards to the Duke's Palace for the night.

Charles laid his hands on the common people the next day as a cure for the king's evil or scrofula; something he would do more than any other king of England during his reign. Afterwards he attended a cathedral service where hymns were sung in his honour. Catherine, as a Catholic, did not attend but she spent the afternoon greeting the people of Norwich and they loved her for it.

I cannot likewise here forbeare to let yu know how infinitely gratious her Majesty was to all our City ; being pleas'd to condiscend so farre as to let allmost all sorts of people (of what degree soever) to kisse her hand, euer as she past along the Gallery, with a most admirable and saintlike charity and patience ; so as our whole inhabitants within & without doores ring & sing of nothing else but her prayses; continuall prayers and teares being offer'd up for her temporall and eternall blessings, by us, whoe all conclude that if ther be a saynt on earth, it must undoubtedly be her Majesty ; since no eye aliue did euer see, nor eare within the memorie of man did euer heare of so much goodnesse, charity, humility, sweetnesse, & virtue of all kindes to meet in one earthly creature, as are now lodged in her Maties saintlike breast.[10]

Catherine's meet and greet was so successful, the mayor presented her with a gift of 400 guineas for her graciousness.

On Michaelmas day the royal couple dined at Blickling Hall, the home of Sir John Hobart and there Charles knighted his thirteen-year-old son, Henry. They then moved on to the home of the Pastons at Oxnead which was commemorated in a poem.

Paston and Hobart did bring up the meat,
Who, the next day, at their own houses treat,
Paston to Oxnead did his sovereign bring,
And, like Arannah, offered as a king.
Blickling two monarchs and two queens has seen;
One king fetched thence — another brought a queen.
Great Townsend, of the treats brought up the rear,
And doubly was my lord-lieutenant there.[11]

There was an oak tree at Oxnead where it was said that Charles and Catherine sheltered under its branches whilst enjoying a game of archery. Catherine was so good that she hit the bullseye! She was patroness of the Honourable Company of Bowmen in London who would later produce 'a silver badge for the marshal of the fraternity...weighing twenty-five ounces, with the figure of an archer, drawing the long English bow to his ear, bearing the inscription, "Regina Catharine Sagitarii," having also the arms of England and Portugal, with two bowmen for supporters'.[12]

After a few more stops on their progress, their majesties returned to Euston Hall. Being close to Newmarket, Charles could indulge his passion for horses and racing. Nell was at Newmarket but pregnant with the king's child and housed away from the other nobles. But another passion was brewing. Louise had been in the queen's entourage and it is said that here in October she finally gave in and slept with the king, even taking part in a mock marriage with him. It is hoped Catherine was not around to see Charles' infatuation flourish. She may have returned to Norwich or London by now especially since the next morning Louise got up in her nightdress and stayed that way throughout the day blatantly advertising her new role as king's mistress.

Catherine returned to Somerset House as the court returned to Whitehall. At Christmas, she heard that Nell, now with her own property in Pall Mall, had given birth to a second son of the king's christened James, on 25 December 1671. Catherine didn't have the strength to be upset. She wasn't well over the winter months and her doctor morbidly proclaimed that she had consumption and wouldn't last the year. He was wrong but Louise hung on every word. She asked for regular reports of the queen, convinced that if Catherine were to die, she would be raised from mistress to royalty.

With a new year came fresh hostilities with the Dutch. Catherine was well enough to want to inspect the English fleet in May. Charles had left her out of his previous visit but wrote to the Duke of York 'I should have no peace at home if I did not permit my wife to go to see the fleet. She will go there tomorrow and a large store of ladies with her'.[13] But as Catherine made her way to Deal, it was reported that the Dutch had been spotted off the Isle of Thanet. This did nothing to put Catherine off and she continued on but with a storm brewing, the Dutch had taken shelter further along the coast at Dover. Catherine and her ladies followed them there the next day and the queen was to witness their enemy's fleet lying out at sea. Back in London, her watermen and barge-masters were ordered to join the king's men and serve on English ships.

The Battle of Solebay near Southwold in Suffolk took place on 7th June. As per the secret treaty of Dover, France came to the aid of England swelling the fleet that sailed to meet the Dutch yet by the time the Duke of York and the Earl of Sandwich had engaged their ships, the French had steered south away from the main battle. There was fierce naval combat, watched from the cliffs by

English folk, who could barely see through the smoke of gunfire. As the battle continued all day, they were ordered to stand fast should the Dutch win and invade England. By the time it ended, both sides were claiming victory. Both sides had lost two ships and around 2,000 men – the English casualties including the Earl of Sandwich. The French had also been engaged and lost two vessels. There was no clear winner and all ships withdrew to safe harbours. Catherine and Charles went to greet the Duke of York once he was back on shore and meet the French captains, listening intently to their battle stories.

Although they were at war, Catherine enjoyed this time with the king. They had always shared a love of the sea and ships and it was something that brought them together. Catherine even had her own frigate, the *Soudades*, captained by James Jennifer. A love of the navy was something she could share with her husband, unlike the gift of children that the king's mistresses were still giving.

In July Louise de Kérouaille gave birth to Charles II's last son, a boy they called Charles – another one named after his father. Lady Castlemaine had also given birth earlier this month but it was probably not the king's – she having moved on to other amours. Charles however, did his duty and acknowledged the baby girl, Barbara Fitzroy. Moll Davis also gave birth later in the year to a daughter, Mary Tudor, the king's last child. With all his mistresses pregnant, Charles had been keeping company with one Winifred Wells, who Pepys once spoke of as 'a great beauty'. This year Charles gave her £2,150 as a dowry for her marriage to Thomas Wyndham. Winifred would later join Catherine's household in Somerset House and become a loyal servant to her as her dresser.

Back in 1672, Charles had put forward his Royal Declaration of Indulgence to promote religious tolerance and pave the way for any move towards making England a Catholic country. The secret treaty of Dover was still undisclosed and Charles had made no public declaration or attempt to change his faith knowing that there would be an uproar. His mother had been Catholic and the Duke of York, his brother, was also known to be Catholic but the time was not right for the king to declare himself.

In March 1673, parliament convinced Charles to withdraw his declaration and to forward a Test Act that ultimately banned Catholics and non-conformists from public service. Only those that took the oaths of supremacy and allegiance and declared against transubstantiation could be employed. James, Duke of York, had to resign as Lord High Admiral and allow Prince Rupert to take his place. Thomas Clifford, Lord Treasurer also resigned and Catherine's household was curtailed with only nine Catholic ladies being allowed in her employ, including Louise. There had also been a move to dismiss Catherine's Catholic priests but as they were Portuguese subjects, they were allowed to stay.

Still her enemies moved against her including Lord Shaftesbury – a man who had fought on both Royalist and Parliamentary sides in the civil war and served under Cromwell. Charles had appointed him to the position of Chancellor of the Exchequer in 1661 and in 1672 he was promoted to Lord Chancellor but he was no friend to Catherine. One of his key goals was the king's divorce and Catherine's replacement with a Protestant queen. He put a motion before parliament that if the king agreed, he should be paid £500,000 but Charles ordered the motion be withdrawn. How many times did he have to tell them he would not divorce his queen? It was the Duke of York who needed to remarry and rumours were rife on who she would be.

Although Louise de Kérouaille clung to dreams of becoming royalty, Charles had no intention of ever supplanting Catherine. Louise delighted him with an impressive ball in July although it didn't turn out quite as expected. 'When the King, Duke and all the young Lords and ladies went up to Barn Elms, and there intended to have spent the evening in a ball and supper amongst those shades, the trees to have been enlightened with torches, ... the report of it brought such a traine of spectators that they were faine to go dance in a barne and sup upon the water'.[14] So what if plans changed, the king was enthralled by his French mistress and later in the year Louise was created Duchess of Portsmouth, Countess of Farnham and Baroness Petersfield. Poor Nell was furious. She had hoped to be given a title herself, perhaps Countess of Plymouth, but her background meant that she would never be ennobled.

Come November there was a new lady on the scene and one that parliament disapproved of. The Duke of York had decided to marry the most devout Mary Beatrice of Modena, a Catholic like himself. She arrived with her mother to no ceremonious fanfare but was rather brought by night to Whitehall and shuffled to a secret door into the palace. Catherine at least had the graciousness to meet her due to her maternal nature and affinity with another foreign princess being brought to a strange land. The queen had left the security of Somerset House to try to ease these ladies into their new surroundings and her job was made all the more difficult by the ladies of the court snubbing the new arrivals.

On a different note, Catherine was further put out when she heard her new Master of Horse, Ralph Montague, had been thrown in the tower. As loyal to Catherine as his brother had been, Ralph challenged the Duke of Buckingham to a duel for rudeness to the queen. Duelling was prohibited and Ralph found himself imprisoned for his chivalry. Charles released him a few days later after he had cooled off. It was a reminder to Catherine though that her enemies still surrounded her at court.

Still Catherine had to return to console the ever fretful Mary Beatrice who had been convinced to marry James. She would have much rather taken her vows and the thoughts of marrying a man twenty-five years older than her was horrific. Catherine often found her weeping but she had been married by proxy to James in Modena in September and now on the 25th November, they were to marry in England. Mary took one look at her bridegroom – James was by now scarred by smallpox – and burst into tears. James, on the other hand, was pleased with his new young wife and introduced her to his step-daughters as their new playfellow. Catherine could only feel for the little Italian princess and wonder what the years to come would bring.

Chapter Six

The Peaceful Years
1674–1677

Catherine continued to help the newly-wed Mary Beatrice of Modena feel comfortable at court. In January 1674, she organised the first Italian opera to be performed in England in honour of Mary and her mother at Somerset House. Catherine had long been a patroness of foreign musicians and it was another way in which she could relax in her own surroundings enjoying the music that she loved.

Although the Venetian ambassador thought the state of English government was lax saying 'The king calls a cabinet council for the purpose of not listening to it and the ministers hold forth in it so as not be understood',[1] a bill was put forward in February that further banned Catholics from sitting in parliament, entering the king's presence or going to court. Catherine and her people as well as the Duke of York and his new wife were the only ones that could be made an exception, yet Catherine didn't go unscathed. The bishops declared that mass could not be said apart from in the Queen's chapel or those of foreign ambassadors. At least she could continue her devotions but the warehouse over her stables was ransacked by those looking for Popish propaganda and a close watch was put on the comings and goings of Somerset House. It was declared that 'fitting persons be appointed to watch for and apprehend'[2] any English man or woman seen going to her chapel.

Under a cloud of suspicion, Catherine was soon to fall ill with nervous headaches and was advised to take the waters at Bath. Louise, who had been ill herself and had already visited Tunbridge Wells, accompanied the queen. The king's mistress was an irritant although Catherine felt some sympathy for her.

Louise's illness was one Charles had given her – the pox – or syphilis as we now know it. With the recent swell of anti-Catholic feeling, the queen's entourage was ignored on their journey and the sheriffs of the counties Catherine passed through didn't ride out to escort her to Bath. Once there, the queen was further snubbed and didn't receive any respectful visits from the town mayor or his aldermen. It prompted Charles to have a reprimand sent 'notice being taken that you were wanting in your duty to Her Majesty in her late passage through your county, to Bath, I am commanded by His Majesty to remind you that you may repair that omission by presenting yourself to the Queen on her return, which will be next week, she intending to set out on Monday, and to lie that night at Marlboro, and the next at Reading, and so to London on the third, according to which you may do your duty to her at some convenient place'[3] but it is unrecorded whether they made amends to Catherine. There was so much ill-will towards Catholics at the time that the queen was openly disrespected. Her trip to Bath hardly provided the cure she sought for her headaches.

From Bath Catherine went to visit Sir Henry Creswicke at Bristol and then joined the king and court at Windsor for the rest of the summer where there was 'a great entertainment at Sir Robert Holme's at Cranbourne Lodge, in the Forest'.[4] There was also much talk of a recent discovery at the Tower of London – could they have found the bodies of Edward IV's sons, the princes in the tower? John Knight, the king's surgeon recorded:

In order to the rebuilding of several Offices in the Tower, and to clear the White Tower from all contiguous building, digging down the stairs which led from the King's Lodgings, to the Chapel in the said Tower, about ten foot in the ground were found the Bones of two striplings in (as it seemed) a wooden chest, which upon the survey were found proportionable to the ages of those two Brothers viz. about thirteen and eleven years. The skull of the one being entire, the

other broken, as were indeed many of the other Bones, also the chest,
by the violence of the laborers, who cast the rubbish and them away
together, wherefore they were caused to sift the rubbish, and by that
means preserved all the bones. The circumstances being often
discoursed with Sir Thomas Chichley, Master of the Ordinance, by
whose industry the new Buildings were then in carrying on, and by
whom this matter was reported to the King[5]

No one knew for sure if the bones were really the princes, but it
gave the court something to ruminate over. Charles certainly
believed they were. He would later have them buried in
Westminster Abbey in a marble urn designed by Christopher
Wren which includes the inscription *Charles II, a most compas-*
sionate prince, pitying their severe fate, ordered these unhappy Princes
to be laid amongst the monuments of their predecessors.

These next few years were peaceful ones for Catherine. She
spent most of her time at Somerset House enjoying her tranquil
gardens that looked over the river and the solitude of her chapel.
She attended the king when required but Charles left her mostly
to her own devices. In December 1674 she ordered a masque to
be performed, *Calisto: or, the Chaste Nymph*, written by Crowe, to
give the Duke of York's daughters, Princesses Mary and Anne an
opportunity to take part. Since the death of their mother they
had spent most of their time at Richmond Palace and Catherine
felt for them. Her caring nature made her want to see them
included more as she had tried to do for their new stepmother,
Mary Beatrice of Modena.

The only thorn in her side was Louise de Kérouaille. She had
accepted her as a Lady of her Bedchamber but on the condition
she rarely attended on her. She had no need for the king's
mistress to be in her presence. Louise, feeling better, after nearly
a year of illness, decided to attend her at dinner, which earnt her
a strict telling-off from the king.

Nell provided some light relief though. She had never taken

to Louise who she thought was stuck up and self-important and took every opportunity to tease her. In December news of the death of the Chevalier de Rohan reached the court and Louise, claiming some dubious family connection, made a show of herself by dressing in mourning clothes and weeping and wailing her way around Whitehall until Charles had her escorted back to her apartments. The next day Nell appeared similarly dressed bemoaning the death of the make-believe Cham of Tartary using all of her actress skills to upstage the king's mistress. When asked what relation the Cham was to Nell, she is reported to have said 'he was as close to me as the chevalier de Rohan was to the Duchess of Portsmouth'[6] thus firmly putting Louise in her place.

In the summer of 1675, Nell delighted the court by performing in a court masque in honour of Philip William, Prince of Neuberg who had arrived in England on a state visit. Dressed as an Arcadian shepherdess, she danced for the gathered crowd and crying out she was too hot, had all the windows opened to let in the cool night air. For once, Catherine and Louise had something in common. Whilst others were glad for the relief, they both sat and shivered. Nell completely took charge of the proceedings and led the prince and her king plus all the other courtiers into St James Park to continue the revelries way into the night.

Talk began in July that the king and Louise's son was to be made Duke of Richmond and Lennox, a title once belonging to Frances Stuart's husband who had died in 1672. Louise was delighted. It was something that she strived for – prestige and promotion and her parents were now living in England, able to witness their daughter and grandson's rise. Lady Castlemaine also wanted her son to take a title and it was agreed he would become Duke of Grafton. But whose son would take precedence? Both women wanted their son created first and they pestered Charles incessantly for his answer. The Lord Treasurer was responsible for signing the patents so it really came down to which one he signed and authorised first. Charles tried to convince the women they could be done at the same time but Louise was well aware that wasn't going to happen. Hearing the treasurer, Lord Danby, was about to head for Bath she sent her attorney over to him the night of his departure leaving Lady Castlemaine to arrive the next day to a locked house. Louise had won this round.

Catherine left them to it and had a more comfortable day in September where the continued good weather saw the court back at Windsor and Catherine headed out to enjoy the sun, away from all the king's mistresses and their demands. At a picnic 'All the Queen's servants treated her by everyone bringing their dish, who then attended her into the forest, and she ate under a tree. Lady Bath's dish was a chine of beef, Mrs Windham's a venison pasty, but Mr Hall brought two dozen of ruffs and reeves and delicate baskets of fruit, Mr Chiffinch, for his daughter's behalf, twelve dozen of choice wine. The Queen wonderfully pleased and merry, and none but herself and her servants'.[7] It was the calm before the storm of the arrival of the king's next mistress.

Hortense Mancini was the niece of the late Cardinal Mazarin, France's chief minister. During the time Charles had been in exile the king-in-waiting had asked for her hand in marriage but her uncle had refused. She had been married off to the religious fanatic, the Duc de la Meilleraye, a jealous and suspicious man who went as far as having his female servants' teeth knocked out to make them unattractive. He even destroyed his own art collection by painting over any bare breasts or exposed flesh and chipped off the pertinent bits from many priceless sculptures. Hortense's rooms were regularly searched for hidden lovers and she was made to spend her days in prayer for forgiveness of her sins – real or otherwise. Under such a regime, Hortense rebelled and began an affair with Sidonie de Courcelles. When her husband found out he had both girls shut in a convent for a time.

Hortense escaped from the duc in 1668 and after travelling in

Europe, disguised as a man, she finally settled down to life as the mistress of the Duke of Savoy. After his death in 1675, his widow asked her to leave their home and Hortense was at a loss as to where to go. The English ambassador to France, Ralph Montagu, suggested she visit her cousin, Mary Beatrice, in London. He was no friend to Louise and hoped that Hortense would capture the king's eye once again and take her place.

She definitely caused a stir, dressed as a Cavalier and with her black pageboy, rescued from a Mediterranean corsair, with only a few other servants in tow. Hortense stayed at first with Lady Elizabeth Harvey in Convent Garden before visiting Mary. Charles, of course, welcomed her as he would do any lady in distress. He arranged for apartments to be made ready for her close to her pregnant cousin and allowed her a pension of £4000 a year. Hortense could now comfortably settle into London society.

The king wasn't immediately infatuated with her but it didn't take him long. Louise still commanded his affections as did Nell but Lady Castlemaine's time as king's mistress was over and she left for France in March 1676 taking four of her children with her. Louise gave birth to a premature baby early in the year and was ill for months. Catherine was happy in her own world and visited John Evelyn's wife at Sayes Court, Deptford in April. He wrote 'My wife entertained her majesty at Deptford, for which the queen gave me thanks, in the withdrawing-room at Whitehall'.[8] It was hard to keep up with the king's mistresses these days – who was in favour, who wasn't – and Catherine stayed away from court, taking her own pleasures elsewhere, while Charles surrounded himself with other women.

When the court moved to Newmarket the king didn't arrange Louise's lodgings and she was forced to rent her own house. To lift her spirits, she took the waters at Bath from 25th May – 4th July and dined with the king at Windsor on her return on the 5th but he didn't ask her to stay the night. Louise was convinced that

Hortense was now a fixture in his life. In Whitehall, Lady Castlemaine had left her apartments and her illegitimate daughter Anne (by Charles) continued to live there. Hortense and Anne began an intimate friendship and Charles used the excuse to see both his daughter and his new mistress at the same time. Anne had married Thomas Lennard, the Count of Sussex at the age of thirteen in August 1674 at Hampton Court. Her husband wanted her to live at his rural ancestral home but she disliked life in the countryside. Instead she stayed at Whitehall and gave birth to her daughter Barbara in July. Visits from Hortense were a pleasure and a distraction from a somewhat boring life. As her father became attracted to the charming Hortense so did Anne, absolutely entranced by this dashing, adventurous lady.

Louise was appalled at the time the king was spending with them, feeling herself to be left out and out of favour. The French ambassador visiting Louise in August reported 'Yesterday evening I saw something which aroused all my pity... I went to see Madame de Portsmouth. She opened her heart to me in the presence of two of her maids...Madame de Portsmouth explained to me what grief the frequent visits of the King of England to Madame de Sussex cause her every day... two girls remained propped against the wall with downcast eyes; their mistress let loose a torrent of tears. Sobs and sighs interrupted her speech. Indeed, I have never beheld a sadder or more touching sight'.[9]

Nell was also put out but as was her way she found humour in the situation telling everyone she was going into mourning for the death of all of Louise's hopes and dreams. The rivalry between the three women was the talk of the court and when they appeared together people delighted in watching any inter-actions between them and most importantly how the king treated them.

Edmund Waller's poem, *The Triple Combat*, captured their

rivalry. It starts:

> *When through the world fair Mazarin had run,*
> *Bright as her fellow-traveller, the sun,*
> *Hither at length the Roman eagle flies,*
> *As the last triumph of her conquering eyes.*
> *As heir to Julius, she may pretend*
> *A second time to make this nation bend;*
> *But Portsmouth, springing from the ancient race*
> *Of Britons, which the Saxon here did chase,*
> *As they great Caesar did oppose, makes head,*
> *And does against this new invader lead.*

And continues with the appearance of Nell as Chloris.

> *Venus had been an equal friend to both,*
> *And victory to declare herself seems loth;*
> *Over the camp, with doubtful wings, she flies,*
> *Till Chloris shining in the field she spies.*
> *The lovely Chloris well-attended came,*
> *A thousand Graces waited on the dame;*
> *Her matchless form made all the English glad,*
> *And foreign beauties less assurance had;*
> *Yet, like the Three on Ida's top, they all*
> *Pretend alike, contesting for the ball...*[10]

Amongst all the gossip and chaos that Hortense had created, Nell wasn't to be left out. She wanted something from the king but it wasn't for herself. It was for her son. She had stood by as other mistress's children were ennobled and now she wanted the same for her eldest child. The story goes that Nell called out to little Charles 'Come hither, you little bastard!'[11] When the king remonstrated with her for such course language she demurely replied that she had no other title to call him by. Her ploy worked and their son was made Baron Heddington and Earl of Burford on 27th December.

Charles was further plagued by his old mistress Lady Castlemaine who still living in Paris had heard of her daughter's affair with Hortense. She inundated him with letters urging him to do something. Although no stranger to scandal herself, Barbara dreaded to think of Anne being the talk of the court especially after hearing that Hortense and Anne had been seen practising their fencing techniques at night in St James Park in their nightgowns. It was actually Anne's husband who retrieved his wife from Whitehall and took her back to their country estate at Herstmonceux in Sussex where she reportedly took to her bed with a picture of Hortense, now fast becoming known as the Italian whore.

Hortense had appeared early in 1677 'raised above all other ladies behind the throne'[12] but it wasn't long before she embarked on an affair with the Prince of Monaco who had arrived in London the previous winter. Charles was so infuriated with her that he stopped her allowance but unable to stick to his guns for long where women were concerned, he renewed payments not long after. The damage was done though. Hortense's brief ascendancy as *'maitresse en titre'* was over and Louise resumed her position. Catherine could only wonder at how the king had the energy to put up with them all.

Another visitor to court came in the autumn. William, Prince of Orange and Charles' nephew, came to marry Princess Mary, the Duke of York's daughter. She was just fifteen, he nearly twenty-seven. Mary was appalled at not only having to marry a man known for being disagreeable and bad-natured but she was desperately frightened at having to leave England to live in Holland. Her father could have been dissuaded from making the match if it wasn't for Charles insisting they make this alliance.

Catherine tried to comfort her but to no avail. Mary was married to the prince on 4th November at St James Palace.

Charles tried to jolly them along by accompanying them to the marriage bed and exclaiming 'Now nephew to your work! Hey St George for England!'[13] but neither of them were in the mood for humour. Mary wept constantly in the days that followed. Catherine tried to cheer her up by moving her birthday celebrations to the 15th instead of the 25th so Mary could take part before the newlyweds left for Holland. No expense was spared and the court came alive with music and dancing yet Mary's sadness could be plainly seen and the Prince of Orange was so unpleasant he earnt the nickname of the 'Dutch Monster', which made her weep all the more. The next days before their departure were painful for Mary and Catherine spent hours trying to console her, telling her she was lucky to have married her husband and be travelling with him for she hadn't even seen Charles and they were strangers when they first met. Catherine explained that it was a princess's role to leave her country and her people behind as she had done. Mary was in no mood to be consoled and snapped 'But, madam, you came into England, and I am leaving England.'[14] On the 21st November, she sailed off to her new life. Catherine felt for her and had tried to do her best to make the situation easier but she was right. A princess, and often a queen, must do as she was told.

Chapter Seven

The Popish Plot
1678–1679

Louise de Kérouaille was seriously ill at the start of the new year. A letter to Lord Rochester reported 'My Lady Portsmouth has been ill to the greatest degree. The King imputes her cure to his dropps, but her confessor to the Virgin Mary, to whom hee is said to have promised in her name that in case of recovery she should have no more commerce with that known enemy to virginity and chastity the monarke of Great Britain, but that she should return to a cloyster in little Brittany and there end her dayes'[1] but Louise wasn't going anywhere.

After such a peaceful few years, 1678 also did not bode well for the queen either. If Catherine had known what was coming, living in a cloister might have been a preferable option for her, never mind Louise. Shaftesbury, the once Lord Chancellor, began agitating again for Charles' divorce. He suggested that if the king declared he had been married to Lucy Walters, the Duke of Monmouth's mother, Catherine could be put aside and the duke could be made his legitimate heir. Charles is supposed to have retorted 'I would rather see James hung up at Tyburn than entertain such a thought!'[2] In January, Charles was forced to make a public declaration that he had never married Lucy but rumours abounded that his former mistress had given their marriage contract to Bishop John Cosin in a black box before her death in 1658. In March, he wrote down his declaration. 'For the voiding of any dispute which may happen in time to come concerning the succession to the Crown, I do here declare in the presence of Almighty God, that I never gave nor made any contract of marriage, nor was married to any woman whatsoever, but to my present wife Queen Catharine now living'[3] but it wouldn't be the last of it.

On the 13th August Charles decided to take his beloved spaniels for a walk in St James Park. His peace was interrupted by one Christopher Kirkby, a sometime employee in the king's laboratory. Charles was used to being approached and usually brushed off advances from people wanting his attention but Kirkby slipped a note into the king's hand and implored him to curtail his walk as he was in immediate danger. Charles didn't take the warning, his dogs yapping at his heels, and he told Kirkby he would talk to him later, continuing on through the park. The king didn't know it yet but this one interaction would be the start of something far bigger and way more sinister.

Kirkby was really being used by Titus Oates and Israel Tonge who between them had contrived the Popish Plot – a supposed plot by Catholics to kill the king. Although completely fictitious, no one knew this at the time and it would increase anti-Catholic sentiment in England to fever point, cause the deaths of many innocent people and plunge Catherine into the most dangerous times of her reign.

Titus Oates had a bad reputation from the start. He had studied at Casius College in Cambridge but was asked to move to St John's from which he left in disgrace in 1669 for inappropriate behaviour. He had found a position as curate in 1673 but his drunken services led him to yet another role as chaplain on a naval vessel from which he was expelled for sodomy. He met Tonge, a schoolteacher and fanatical clergyman around 1677, and not long after converted to the Catholic faith. He was sent to the English college in Valladolid in Spain to learn theology but was again asked to leave and was then expelled from the college in St Omer several months later. He was a dubious character, a man not to be trusted but he would become first and foremost in revealing the so-called plot in the coming months.

Israel Tonge had been living in lodgings at the Barbican and when Oates visited him there telling him he knew of a plot to kill the king, Tonge urged him to write it all down. Oates hid a copy of his writings in the wainscot near Tonge's lodgings for him to 'find' and Kirkby was set up to read the manuscript and be convinced to tell the king he was in danger.

Charles received Kirkby later the same day and asked him to explain himself for such a rude and abrupt interruption to the king's daily walk. He was told that two men, Thomas Pickering and John Grove, were planning to shoot him and failing that the queen's physician would poison him. Charles was sceptical and asked for the source of his information. Tonge was brought in and began reading Oates' manuscript that contained forty-three allegations but was interrupted by the impatient king who said he would pass the matter to Lord Danby, his trusted advisor.

Danby conducted a private investigation into the matter and tried to find the men, Pickering and Grove, but to no avail. Tonge and Oates stepped up their game by trying to implicate Father Bedingfield, the Duke of York's Catholic confessor, to whom they had sent five letters from supposed plotters but the priest had already taken the letters to the duke sensing he was being set up. It was clear the letters were forgeries but the duke demanded a public inquiry thus catapulting the plot into the limelight.

On 6th September Oates went to the magistrate Sir Edmund Berry Godfrey to swear an oath to the truth of his allegations and by the 28th Oates and Tonge were called to explain it all to the Privy Council. Oates then read out his allegations in full. The Catholics were planning to rise up and slaughter all the Protestants in England. The king would be killed and the pope would give control of the country to the Jesuits. This was being planned by Catholic nobles and members of religious orders. It reached into the court with Sir George Wakeman, Catherine's physician, and Edward Coleman, once the Duchess of York's secretary, named as main conspirators.

On 12th October, Sir Edmund Berry Godfrey went missing and was found dead in a ditch at Primrose Hill impaled on his own sword on the 17th. For the people it was proof of a Catholic plot and it added to mounting hysteria brought on by Oates' allegations. An anti-Catholic mob attended the magistrate's funeral as the city's fury and fear grew.

Oates layered on his stories. The great fire of London had been the Catholic's doing. There were five nobles who were involved in the plot. And then there was Catherine, the king's own wife who wished her husband dead. Oates enlisted a felon named Bedloe who had made his acquaintance in Spain to bring about suspicion on the queen. He testified that Sir Edmund Berry Godfrey had been murdered by Catherine's servants and his 'corpse was laid on the High Altar of the Queen's chapel'[4] but the next day his story had changed to 'the murder was committed by the Queen's popish servants at Somerset House...that he saw the body there, lying on the Queen's back-stairs, that it lay there two days, and he was offered two thousand guineas to help remove it. That at last it was removed at nine o'clock at night, by some of the queen's people'.[5]

Charles didn't believe the queen was in any way involved. In fact, he had been with her at the times Bedloe had stated. He ordered the man to show the Duke of York where exactly he had supposedly seen the body. Bedloe pointed out a passageway but it was one regularly used by Catherine's servants and guarded by her footmen. There was no way a body had lain there for two days. Still a search of Somerset House was ordered which turned up nothing sinister. Charles could see where this was going. Already a Mrs Elliott had gained an audience with him to ask that he meet with Oates in private to discuss matters concerning the queen. Charles dismissed the woman saying 'I will never suffer an innocent lady to be oppressed'.[6] Catherine was in danger and he asked her to return to her apartments in Whitehall so that she would be under his protection.

At the beginning of November though Titus Oates received a general pardon for 'all treasons, felonies, misdemeanours committed before 1 Nov., 1678, and all fines or penalties by reason thereof, whether he be indicted, convicted or condemned for the same or not, with restitution of lands and goods'.[7] He was the man of the hour, some felt even a hero to have exposed such a plot to assassinate their king and he still had it in for Catherine.

On 13th November Oates had an audience with the king. He was questioned as to what he knew of Catherine's involvement with the conspirators. He had to admit that he 'never saw any of the Queen's letters to them, but of theirs to her acknowledging her favours &c. he has seen'. He did know that Catherine had given the Jesuits, members of the Catholic church, money. On one occasion £4,000 for which they returned the Queen '500 masses, 650 pair of beads, 1,150 mortifications'.[8] She had two Jesuits priests, he said, but could not say they were involved in the plot.

As Oates previous conversation with the king had not got him anywhere, he now formally charged Catherine with conspiring with her physician to poison the king. Oates testified:

That in the preceding July, he saw a letter, in which it was affirmed by sir George Wakeman, the queen's catholic physician, that her majesty had been brought to give her assent to the murder of the king ; that, subsequently, one sir Richard, or sir Robert, of Somerset House, evidently pointing at sir Richard Bellings, the queen's secretary, came with a message from her majesty for certain jesuits to attend her, with whom, one day in August, he went to Somerset House...They went into her majesty's closet, leaving him in the antechamber, the door of which these clever plotters were so obliging as to leave ajar, in order to enable him to hear the discourse which, he pretended, passed between them and the queen...He heard a female voice exclaim, 'I will no longer suffer such indignities to my bed I am content to join in procuring his death and the propagation of the catholic faith,' and that 'she would assist sir George Wakeman in poisoning the king... that when the jesuits came out, he requested to see the queen, and had, as he believed, a gracious smile of her majesty; and while he was within, he heard the queen ask father Harcourt 'whether he had received the last 10,000l' and, as far as he could judge, it was the same voice which he had heard when he was in the ante-room, and he saw no other woman there but the queen.[9]

Oates was carefully questioned and also told to point out the place where this had happened and, as Bedloe had done, he got the rooms wrong. But Bedloe added testimony to Oates charge. He too said he had heard the queen conspiring with Jesuits. When asked why he hadn't told them of this when he was questioned over the death of Sir Edmund Berry Godfrey, he said it had slipped his memory.

Catherine put on a brave face despite these accusations. Evelyn recorded that the queen still held her birthday celebrations 'I never saw the court more brave, nor the nation in more apprehension and consternation...Oates grew so presumptuous as to accuse the queen of a design to poison the king, which certainly that pious and virtuous lady abhorred the thoughts of, and Oates's circumstances made it utterly unlikely, in my opinion. He probably thought to gratify some who would have been glad his majesty should have married a fruitful lady; however, the king was too kind a husband to let any of these make impression on him'.[10]

Bedloe and Oates were called to the bar of the House of Commons on 28th November. Oates stepped forward and declared 'I, Titus Oates, do accuse Queen Catherine of conspiring the king's death and contriving how to compass it'.[11] The house erupted with the news but not in defence of Catherine. Many there believed the queen, as a Catholic and part of the plot, was capable of such a crime. There were suggestions she should be removed from Whitehall and sent back to Portugal or taken to the Tower for interrogation. The members of the Commons sent for the Lords but they weren't as easily swayed. Why should the queen be imprisoned on the word of men like Oates and Bedloe? Even Oates admitted afterwards 'I do not think we are ready yet for impeaching the queen'.[12] Oates and Bedloe thought Catherine would be an easy target and that the king would fail to protect her. He could even use the plot as an excuse to put aside his barren queen but Charles as ever stood by his loyal wife.

Life for Catherine now was miserable and she lived in constant apprehension, waiting for the next move against her. Many of her Catholic servants left in November and when she went out she was booed and hissed at by the people. Her only true support came from Charles and she was grateful to him. She could at least rely on her husband.

Trials of eminent Catholics continued and five peers – Lords Arundel, Belassis, Powys, Stafford and Petre – were sent to the Tower. Bedloe still hadn't finished with implicating the queen either. He now blamed Miles Prance, a silversmith, who cleaned the plate in Catherine's chapel for the death of Sir Edmund Berry Godfrey. Prance, probably hoping for a pardon, admitted his guilt and named three of the queen's servants as the perpetrators of the magistrate's demise. He said that two of them, Green and Hill, lured Godfrey to an alleyway where Berry awaited and between them 'they strangled him and broke his neck'.[13] They would be hanged at Tyburn early the next year.

Catherine knew that her brother Pedro in Portugal had heard of the situation in England. In fact, the entire country knew and were horrified at the way in which their princess was being treated. In Lisbon, mobs gathered around the houses of English residents looking for vengeance. Pedro had to deal with the city's unrest but was more concerned for his sister and began to plan to have her escorted back to Portugal.

Catherine wrote to him:

Her Majesty hath borne with a great deal of patience many incon-veniences but now her patience is quite tired out, seeing herself accused of consenting to the death of the King; and she has only this to bear her up, that His Majesty continues his wonted kindnesses to her, and that he and the nobility also are so far from believing the accusation that they have imprisoned the accuser, and therefore she thinks it necessary to advise His Highness, that he may understand and afford her his advice and assistance in these straits[14]

Charles also deemed it necessary to write to Catherine's brother.

We doubt not but that Your Highness hath already heard of the unhappy reflexion that hath lately been raised against our Dear Consort, the Queen, and do believe Your Highness hath taken a sensible part with Us in that indignation wherewith we have resented the same. We brought the matter (as soon as it was known) into our Council Board, and the reception which it had there, We are sure will not sound unpleasing to Your Highness, because it gave satisfaction to Us, and did let the Queen clearly see that all was done for her present vindication which the time would permit. But this misfortune arising while the States of our Kingdom were assembled, who by their constitution may take cognizance of whatever happens of an extraordinary nature, they drew enquiry before them. And even then such of them as took time to deliberate and to consider how the Queen hath lived, found motives to reject the complaint and instead of favouring the accusation at the time was only spent in magnifying her virtues...[15]

The king went on to praise the virtues of Count Castelmelhor who had been acting as Catherine's advisor but Pedro had sent the man into exile for supporting his deposed brother Alphonso and was in no mood to grant Charles' request that he be allowed to return to Portugal. He did however see the need for Catherine to come home, out of harm's way, and arranged for the Marquis de Arouches to sail to collect her.

In February 1679, Francis Parry, the English minister to the court of Portugal wrote:

> Though the Commons should proceed no further in the Queen's accusation, nay, though it prove but a groundless calumny, or that the accusers in satisfaction to her Majesty should be punished with the utmost severity, yet I perceive that the Commons wish her in Portugal, and she has little reason to desire to remain in England, and the other day, being at the Corte Real, one about the Prince, being a sober man, was saying to me that it were best for Her Majesty, seeing she is like to have no children, to return hither, and put herself in the Sacramento, which if you will remember is a convent on the left hand, a little before you come to the great gate that goes to Alcantara, a nunnery of a very strict order, where persons of the best quality, and whither the Marquesa de Mira lately retired, to which nunnery the Queen hath been of late a benefactor. And the same person added that the ambassador that was to go to England was not to stay above two or three months, whence he concluded that the Queen would return with him, for that it was not likely His Highness would leave Her Majesty in England after the broils...'[16]

It seems like everyone had plans for Catherine but as she had made clear before, she would not enter a nunnery. If the situation grew any more dangerous she may consider leaving for Portugal or France as Charles had suggested but her place was with her king and she was determined to stay with him.

Meanwhile the Duke of York was also feeling the Catholic backlash. Charles sent him to Brussels saying it was 'for my service and your own good'.[17] A bill to exclude him from the succession because of his faith was introduced in May but the king dissolved parliament before it could be passed. Many supported Charles' illegitimate son, the Duke of Monmouth, as the next successor to the throne but the king was adamant that the succession would remain unchanged. It was a fight that would consume parliament for the next few years.

Catherine had her own battle on her hands. The Marquis de Arouches arrived to take her back to Portugal and she refused to go. England had become her home and Charles, for better or for worst, her husband. She felt that her place was beside him come what may. Arouches tried his best to convince her to return to Portugal and when his arguments met with stubborn resistance, he suggested that Pedro would be mightily displeased with her if she did not consent to his will. He was constantly haranguing her and she tired of him and the way he treated her.

Catherine wrote an emotional letter to her brother:

On every occasion that the Marquis has spoken to me I have understood from him that doubts are raised of my good will to you. As this trouble touches me to the quick, I have no patience whatever with it. Yesterday he gave me good cause for grief, and left me in such a way that the King and all the court could not but perceive the annoyance he gave me by reading a paper he said was yours. I doubt this, because I know the writing and the style seem to me very different from others I have seen, but it was enough for me to hear that it was yours, for me to give it my entire attention, and to desire to fail not in anything that was your pleasure. This is manifest, and if he consults his conscience he will make clear to you what I replied, or will relate it accurately. But he speaks to me in terms so different from those my replies merit, that he gives me cause for pain, as I have told you, and because I fear he may dare to write to you in the same doubtful manner as that in which he dared to speak in my presence, I am obliged to give this explanation, that the truth may be clearly known.

I have no need of praise from the marquis, but it is very degrading to me that you doubt me. The King will speak on my behalf, and as many know me, who know there is no one on earth whom I value more highly than the Prince of Portugal, my brother. By the chastisement of God, I have been forced to give evidence of the truth of what I did not think has been doubted. But it is your minister who has done these services to you and me, and forces me to demonstrations such as no slanders whatever, laid upon me by my enemies, compelled me to do till now. It has been observed at court, and they have not done wondering at the cause. They infer the excess of my love for you from it, which I see the marquis doubts.

It seems you are practising to take away my life with pure grief, and the nation thinks that she whom they see so lowered by slander can do little to serve you. I unburden myself to you in this letter, and for my comfort I hope you will send me good news of yourself, which will always arrive at the right time, since it is for that I always long.[18]

We don't know how Pedro replied but Arouches must have received orders to stop harassing the queen. She refused point blank to leave England and instead tried to leave her troubles behind as she retired to Windsor with the king, enjoying the calm and serenity of the park and time in her husband's company.

But she would need his support again soon as Sir George Wakeman, her physician, was brought to trial. Charles had met with the main accusers including Oates and Bedloe before the trial started to find out what evidence they had about the queen. There was nothing concrete, just rumours that Catherine had known about the plot to poison the king. Still Wakeman and three priests were indicted for high treason on 18th July 1679. Oates swore he had seen a letter written by Wakeman detailing the plot and further evidence that if the doctor killed the king he would be made physician-general to the army. But Oates had failed to identify Wakeman or his handwriting. He mentioned the queen only briefly and no more was said on any royal involvement in the plot. Lord Chief Justice William Scroggs picked holes in all the witnesses' statements and summed up by addressing the jury. 'We would not, to prevent all their plots (let them be as big as they can make them), shed one drop of innocent blood; therefore I would have you, in all these gentlemen's cases, consider seriously and weigh truly the circumstances and the probability of things charged upon them'.[19] The jury found Wakeman and the priests not guilty. Their innocence may have been proven but the people weren't convinced, amassing outside their homes and forcing them to flee for safety. Wakeman headed to Whitehall where he asked Charles' and Catherine's permission visited to leave England. It was duly granted in the hopes that the furore around conspiracies and plots to kill the king would die down.

But it was only a matter of time before fresh accusations were levelled at the queen. This time Buss, the Duke of Monmouth's cook, made fresh claims about Catherine's chapel servants being involved in yet another plot. He told Shaftesbury and the Privy Council 'being at Windsor in September last, he heard one Hankinson, who had belonged to the queen's chapel, desire Antonio, the queen's confessor's servant, to have a care of the four Irishmen he had brought along to do the business for them'[20] – the business of killing the king. Antonio was arrested and questioned. Shaftesbury also wanted to interrogate the queen but Charles refused to allow him anywhere near her and the accusation went no further.

Then suddenly to add to the panic of the past months, Charles fell ill. Immediately people began to talk of poison. Here was a plot unfolding. After all the accusations and trials of innocent people, someone had finally found a way to kill the king. The Duke of York was sent for, amidst fear over the succession but Charles rallied. There was no plot, no poisoning. He just had a fever, was treated with quinine and recovered before the duke even arrived.

Catherine was by his side as they left the city and all its rumours and slander for the pleasure of Newmarket and the races in September. They spent so much time together that the comment was passed that Catherine 'is a mistress now, the passion her spouse has for her is so great'.[21] Trials and tribulations had thrown the king and queen together and through such adversity their relationship grew.

Chapter Eight

Conspiracy and Exoneration
1680–1683

In April of 1680 Charles was once again forced to declare he had never married Lucy Walter, the Duke of Monmouth's mother. It was a rumour that just didn't want to go away and Catherine must have been heartily sick of it. When the king had made his previous declaration, this marriage contract was supposed to be in a black box given to Bishop John Cosin before Lucy's death. Since then the mysterious black box was supposed to have passed to Sir Gilbert Gerard, Cosin's son-in-law. The Privy Council called an extraordinary meeting and Gerard was brought in for questioning but he denied all knowledge of a black box or a marriage contract, much to Catherine's relief.

During the past months, Catherine's life had been a series of ups and downs focused on by plotters and defended by the king. At least it had brought them closer. Charles' mistresses had been keeping a low profile, Louise especially, and Catherine was glad that for once they were causing her no grief.

As a Catholic, Louise had feared the attention of the plotters might turn to her. Apart from being named as one who should leave the city along with all the other Catholics no accusations had affected her and she had kept herself busy with political intrigues whilst also planning a quick escape to France should she need to go. But storm clouds were gathering. The people as much as they were trying to bring Catherine down detested Louise even more. A rhyme showed their dislike:

Portsmouth, that pocky bitch,
A damned papistical drab,
An ugly, deformed witch,

Eaten up with the mange and scab.

This French hag's pocky bum
So powerful is of late,
Although it's blind and dumb,
It rules both Church and State.[1]

And Louise had her enemies. Early in 1680 a tract entitled *Articles of High Treason and Other High Crimes and Misdemeanours against the Duchess of Portsmouth* was published. It listed all her supposed crimes including her involvement in the Popish Plot and even an attempt 'to poison the king with the aid of a French confectioner'.[2] Her enemies wanted her impeached and in the summer, Shaftesbury accompanied by seven Whig lords indicted the Duke of York for being a Popish recusant before a grand jury and added that Louise was a 'national nuisance'[3] and nothing more than a common prostitute. Lord Chief Justice William Scroggs, who had presided over the Wakeman trial, dismissed the jury before they had time to make any decision. Louise had escaped the stocks and was safe for now.

Nell Gwyn, as a Protestant and the people's favourite, had nothing to fear from the Popish plotters and she started the year delighted with a gift from Charles of the newly built Burford House in Windsor next to the royal park. But in May and June Nell was ill, some said with a dose of the pox, and when news came of her youngest son's death at his boarding school in Paris, she was utterly devastated. Charles shared in her grief and urged her to focus on her new house. There was still work to be done and rooms to be decorated. Nell threw herself into making the house a hive of activity and a meeting place for her theatrical friends, writers like Edmund Waller and Aphra Behn, and for entertaining rich nobles.

Catherine was also affected by deaths during the summer. Her lord chamberlain, the Earl of Ossory died and was greatly lamented. Catherine took the time to write a personal condolence to his father. 'I do not think any thing I can say will lessen your trouble for the death of my lord Ossory, who is so great a loss to the king and the public, as well as to my own particular service, that I know not how to express it; but every day will teach me, by showing me the want I shall find of so true a friend. But I must have so much pity upon you as to say little on so sad a subject...'.[4]

But one death not so lamented and which in fact brought the queen a huge sense of relief was the death of Bedloe, Oates co-conspirator. On his death bed, he sent for Lord Chief Justice North and swore that all he had said concerning the Popish Plot was true but guilt overtook him. He called the man back and declared that the Duke of York and the Queen were blameless. Catherine's only fault was to want England to be a Catholic nation – which at least publicly wasn't true but the main thing was 'she was ignorant of any design against the king, nor any way concerned in his murder'. Surely Catherine could feel a sense of peace now.

Not yet, for there was more trouble in the autumn when Shaftesbury once more brought the Exclusion Bill to parliament just to see it thrown out again with sixty-three votes to thirty but he didn't stop there. Before the House of Lords he reiterated his wish to see Catherine removed from the throne 'as the sole remaining chance of security, liberty and religion, a bill of divorce might pass, which, by separating the King from Queen Catherine, might enable him to marry a Protestant consort, and thus leave the crown to legitimate issue'.[5] Charles would have none of it and visited the peers to ask them to vote against another slight on his queen and this too was thrown out.

Catherine, her spirits low, succumbed to illness. It plagued her on and off for four months. She wrote to her brother Pedro:

I still go on with very troublesome medicines, and with repeated chills and fevers for eighteen and sixteen hours, which leave me very weak, and from the rigour of the weather I do not know if I shall recover health. As to the state of things in this kingdom, you will have heard everything if they keep you informed as is proper. For my part there is nothing that concerns me more than to tell you how completely the King releases me from all trouble in my private affairs by the care which he takes to defend and protect my innocence and truth. Every days he shews more clearly his purpose and goodwill towards me, and he thus baffles the hate of my enemies. During my illness the esteem in which he holds my safety and life is witnessed by many testimonies of tenderness for which may God give him payment in the same coin, in which case I shall benefit as well. I cannot cease telling you what I owe to his benevolence, of which each day he gives greater proofs, either from generosity, or from compassion for the little happiness in which he sees I live.[6]

But there was no time for the sick bed at the end of November. Lord Stafford, one of the five Catholic lords arrested in the early days of the Popish Plot came to trial. He had spent two years in the Tower and was nearly seventy. He was accused of the same accusations that had been levelled at Catherine – that of plotting to kill the king and bringing Catholicism to England. Catherine needed to see what would happen. She watched the proceedings in Westminster Hall sitting in a private box with her ladies listening to witnesses give statements that often referred to her including how 'the duke of York, the queen, and the chief of the nobility, were in the plot'.[7] Stafford was convicted 'on testimony that ought not to have been taken on the life of a dog'[8] and sentenced to a traitor's death which Charles insisted was changed to beheading. If he couldn't stop the execution he could at least be lenient. It was a stark warning to Catherine who could have easily have been in Stafford's place if it weren't for the king.

On the 12th December, Evelyn wrote 'I saw a meteor of an

obscure bright colour, very much in shape like the blade of a sword... what this may portend God only knows...'[9] Many others echoed his thoughts and Catherine hoped with all her heart that for once it would be a good omen to herald in a new year.

It was not to be for early in 1681 fresh accusations were levelled at the queen and the Duke of York. Catherine must have wondered when this would ever end. This time, Edward Fitzharris, one of the Duchess of Portsmouth's men, published a pamphlet, *A True Englishman Speaking Plain English in a Letter from a Friend to a Friend* that brought the succession into question again and libelled both the king and his brother. Fitzharris also claimed that Francisco de Mello had told him 'that her majesty was engaged in the design of poisoning the king'.[10] Charles refused to have his queen and brother called into question one more time and had Fitzharris indicted for treason. The tide was turning. No longer would Charles listen to his nearest and dearest being accused but he would see that the accuser would be brought to trial.

Charles and Catherine left the city for Windsor on 14th March escorted by a troop of Horse Guards and were closely followed by Shaftesbury and his ever increasing entourage. He even boasted that he had 10,000 'brisk boys of London'[11] to do his bidding should the tide turn against him. Parliament was to be convened on the 21st at Oxford and Shaftesbury was determined that Fitzharris' accusations would be heard. He was still determined to bring Catherine down by any means he could.

Although the royals must have felt a sense of trepidation, they put on a show for the crowds that had gathered to see them enter Oxford. Louise and Nell accompanied them and they spent a few pleasant days before parliament opened being entertained at the university. Charles was not going to let Shaftesbury win. He opened parliament in state and sat back whilst the Exclusion Bill and Fitzharris' trial were fiercely debated. Shaftesbury and his party wanted Fitzharris' case heard in parliament (so they would have a chance of attacking the duke and queen) whilst the Lords ruled he should be tried by a jury of his peers. Charles let the debate rage on for six days and then ordered the Black Rod to summon the Commons. He surprised them all by appearing in full state dress. Sitting on his throne in full regalia, he placed his crown on his head and told them that 'proceedings begun so ill could end in no good'[12] and announced that Parliament was now dissolved. Fitzharris would stand trial in court and Catherine would be safe.

In June Fitzharris was charged with high treason and his trial began. Louise de Kérouaille, Duchess of Portsmouth, was called in as a witness. Louise was absolutely mortified to be involved and told the jury 'I have nothing at all to say to Mr Fitzharris, nor was concerned in any sort of business with him. All I have to say is he desired me to give a petition to the King to get his estate in Ireland, and I did three or four times speak to the King about it. But I have not anything else to say to him'.[13] After more evidence was given though, Louise did finally address him. 'Mr Fitzharris, if I had anything in the world to do you good, I would do it; but I have not, and so can't see that I am any ways more useful here'[14] and with that she left the court. In the end Fitzharris was sentenced to hang at Tyburn but not before he had implicated others.

After his execution, six Irish witnesses, five of whom were Protestant, came forward to give evidence against Shaftesbury. There was finally proof that he had been behind false accusations against Catherine and the Duke of York. He was arrested in July on charges of high treason and sent to the Tower. The queen however had been exonerated and now Catherine could breathe a huge sigh of relief. The plotting against her was over. She had done nothing to harm the king, her protector, and he had done everything to save her from all the false accusations. In October, her arch enemy Oates was arrested for sedition, fined £100,000 and thrown into prison. Perhaps now they could settle into an untroubled life.

In January 1682 the Moroccan ambassador and his richly dressed men wearing turbans and carrying scimitars, visited to discuss Tangier. Catherine and Charles gracefully received them in the Banqueting House at Whitehall with Louise de Kérouaille making a point of organising their entertainment. The king had been unhappy with Louise's involvement in the Fitzharris trial and she was doing her best to remain in his favour. In any case here was a man who brought exotic goods with him; gifts of jewels and silks, two lions and thirty ostriches! Evelyn wrote:

> *This evening, I was at the entertainement of the Morocco Ambassador at the Dutchesse of Portsmouth's glorious apartments at Whitehall, where was a greate banquet of sweetmeats and musiq, but at which both the Ambassador and his retinue behav'd themselves with extraordinary moderation and modesty...*[15]

Nell Gwyn was also at the banquet and the king's daughters by Lady Castlemaine as well as unspecified 'concubines' as Evelyn put it. Catherine seems to have been absent but had quipped 'the mistresses govern all' before returning to her apartments.[16] She was content to leave them. So used to Charles's women was she by now, it was a welcome relief to leave them to long nights of partying whilst she enjoyed the peace of Somerset House. She still enjoyed days out with Charles, sometimes accompanied by the other women, but days where they could enjoy each other's company. One such event was the launch of the *Britannia* at Chatham, a 100-gun naval ship.

Louise was ill in March and desperate for a break, she left England to take the waters in Bourbon taking seventy servants with her. She received a rich welcome at the Paris court on her way there and was given rooms in the palace of Saint-Cloud, attending fetes and festivals before going on to take the medicinal waters, a course of treatments and regular baths in the thermal spring.

Catherine had more time with Charles when they took to Newmarket for the races in May. Nell went with them and kept the king occupied in the evenings. But they were both worried when the king came down with ague though he customarily shrugged it off. It was a pleasant summer and even Louise's return in July couldn't spoil it.

Catherine was happier than she had been in years. She wrote to her brother Pedro:

> ...I am happy, except that I have had no opportunity of procuring news of you...I have everything that can give me complete satisfaction in this life, nor do I now wish to think I have reason to complain...[17]

The poet Waller wrote an ode to her to celebrate the New Year in 1683.

> What revolutions in the world have been!
> How are we changed since first we saw the queen!
> She, like the sun, doth still the same appear,
> Bright as she was on her arrival here.
> Time had commission mortals to impair,
> But things celestial is obliged to spare.
> May every New Year find her still the same
> In health and beauty, as she hither came![18]

Although he was being kind by saying Catherine still appeared the same, the past years had brought her many troubles but at least now life had settled down. Charles was building a palace at Winchester and Catherine spent days here with the king in simple lodging rooms in the town while he oversaw its construction. Her old enemy Shaftesbury had died in Holland after fleeing England the previous November. With him it was felt that the plots against Catherine and the king would die also.

It was a sense of security that would soon be shattered when another plot to kill the king and his brother, the Duke of York, was discovered. Rye House near Hoddesdon, Hertfordshire, was en route to Newmarket and the home of one Captain Richard Rumbold. He, along with many others, planned to waylay the king and his brother on the way back from the races. One hundred men were to be concealed in the grounds and the royal pair would have no chance to escape their assassins. But their plans were foiled when a fire broke out in Newmarket, rushing through the town, and forcing the races to be cancelled. Charles and James returned to Whitehall earlier than expected and the plot had no time to change its plans.

The plotters however had thought of a plan B which centred on the organising of uprisings throughout England and Scotland in effect creating another civil war, but this all came to light in June when an informer confessed and implicated those responsible. By default, this included the Duke of Monmouth, Charles' son, who the plotters had planned would be the next king. Charles was tired of his wayward child and the constant trouble he brought him. Furious that he might have been involved in his planned regicide, he wondered if now it was time to make an example of him, but Catherine interceded on Monmouth's behalf. She had always liked the boy and was tender to all of his mistresses' children. She could not stand by and see Monmouth executed. When a grand jury implicated him in the plot she told Charles that if he didn't do something, his son's life might be forfeit. Monmouth was in hiding but the king got a message to him that he would be pardoned if he came forward and made his confession. The dutiful son, to save his own skin, did precisely that and swore he had no part in the plot to take his father's life but that he did have a part in further conspiracy – that of causing an uprising. Then he changed his mind and wanted to take back his confession. Charles unable to control his temper any more raged at his son and exiled him from court. He had done all he could for him and if that wasn't enough then he could just get out of his sight. And out of England.

Catherine put on a brave front. No one would ruin her long sought after peace and gained sense of tranquillity. She took to late evening walks in the park with Lady Arlington who was roused from a dinner with the diarist Evelyn one night at 11pm to accompany the queen. And there were plans to be made for the Princess Anne's wedding to Prince George of Denmark. Anne was the Duke of York's second eldest daughter by Anne Hyde. She had seen her sister married off to William, Prince of Orange in 1677 and now it was her turn. But as her sister had wept and wailed at the thoughts of marrying, Anne was placid and happy perhaps because she was staying on at Whitehall with her new husband who commented 'We talk here of going to tea, of going to Winchester, and everything else except sitting still all summer, which was the height of my ambition. God send me a quiet life somewhere for I shall not be long able to bear this perpetual motion'.[19] Sentiments Catherine could well echo.

Chapter Nine

Happiness and Disaster
1684–1685

Catherine had mourned the passing of her deposed brother Alphonso at the end of 1683 and the court had shown their respect by wearing mourning clothes throughout the winter. The season was a severe one; so cold that the Thames froze over, temporarily stopping trade, but giving the people a chance to have a frost fair on the river. Catherine and Charles left Whitehall together to attend the festivities, walking amongst the stalls and admiring the whole ox roasting on a solid Thames. Sixteen eighty-four was to be the year of companionship for them. The plots were behind them and they could relax into each other's company, enjoying trips to Winchester, Windsor and Newmarket, walks in St James Park and games of ombre and quadrille in the evenings.

Catherine's birthday in November was celebrated with even more extravagance than usual. Evelyn was amazed by what he saw:

...there were fireworks on the Thames before Whitehall, with pageants of castles, forts, and other devices of girandolas, serpents, the King and Queen's arms and mottoes, all represented in fire...But the most remarkable was the several fires and skirmishes in the very water, which actually moved a long way, burning under the water, now and then appearing above it, giving reports like muskets and cannon, with grenades and innumerable other devices. It is said it cost £1,500. It was concluded with a ball, where all the young ladies and gallants danced in the great hall. The court had not been so brave and rich in apparel since his Majesty's Restoration.[1]

It was to be the last birthday Catherine would spend with Charles. The king was troubled with a sore leg and had curtailed his long strolls in the park taking more to the company of mistresses past and present. Evelyn saw him in the company of Barbara, Louise and Hortense one evening in January gambling and listening to music with much 'luxurious dallying and profaneness'.[2] The next day Charles was suffering from his over-indulgence and visiting Louise asked for a bowl of spoon meat – a type of soupy porridge – but he was unable to eat it and instead settled for a cup of chocolate. He spent the night groaning, complaining of a heaviness in his stomach and around his heart. His servants noticed he appeared lethargic and distracted the next morning and as he was being shaved by his barber he collapsed, his face blackened and distorted. It was treason to bleed the king without a direct order but Dr King seeing his dire condition began the treatment.

Catherine was called for and was closely followed by the Duke and Duchess of York who later recalled 'I hastened to the chamber as soon as I was informed of his majesty's state. I found there, the queen, the duke of York (who is now king), the chancellor, and the first gentleman of the bed-chamber. It was a frightful spectacle, and startled me at first. The king was in a chair — they had placed a hot iron on his head, and they held his teeth open by force. When I had been there some time, the queen, who had hitherto remained speechless, came to me, and said, 'My sister, I beseech you to tell the duke, who knows the king's sentiments with regard to the Catholic religion as well as I do, to endeavour to take advantage of some good moments.'[3] These words would lead to the suggestion that Catherine was responsible for Charles' death bed conversion.

Catherine then fainted and had to be escorted to her rooms. When Charles regained consciousness, she was the first person he asked for. For the moment she was unable to return to him and sent a message begging his pardon. Charles exclaimed 'She begs my pardon! I beg hers with all my heart.'[4]

The king was continuously nursed for two days, if the term nursed really applies. His doctors bled, purged, cupped and cauterised their king. It was estimated 'fifty-eight drugs were administered over five days'.[5] Charles' body was subjected to treatment after treatment in an effort to save his life. Catherine spent as much time at his bedside as she could in between feeling faint and feeling uneasy herself, and then the king seemed to rally, the bells rung out, and fires were lit across the city in celebration that Charles was well.

But the next day it was obvious to all that the king had taken a turn for the worst. He was surrounded by his loved ones, men of office and bishops from across the country. Bishop Ken read the prayers for the sick and dying and asked Charles if he repented his sins. The king responded he did. When he was asked if he would take Holy Communion as well he said 'there will be time enough for that'.[6]

Those closest to him knew he would want to die in the Catholic faith. There had been rumours that Charles had converted over the years as well as the stipulation in the secret treaty with King Louis in which he agreed to become Catholic but the lengths his family went to to get a priest to him shows that this was one of his final acts.

The French ambassador Barillon visited Louise in her chambers to tell her the king was not far from death. As the king's mistress she had no place in his sick room but she was aware of Charles desire to die a Catholic. She told Barillon:

I am going to tell you the greatest secret of the world, and my head would be the price if they knew it! The King is a catholic at the bottom of his heart, but he is surrounded by Protestant Bishops, and no one tells him the state he is in, or speaks to him of God. I cannot with decency enter the room; besides the Queen is there nearly always. The Duke of York thinks of his own affairs, and he has too

many to take that care of the King's conscience which he ought to
do. Go and say to him, that I have conjured you to warn him to
think of what must be done to save the soul of the King. He is master
in the room; he can make any one he likes go out. Lose no time, for
if one delays only a little, it will be too late![7]

Barillon spoke to both the duke and Catherine but Catherine was in no state to help, overcome with tiredness and exhaustion and being bled herself. The Duke of York hurried into Charles and whispered in his ear 'Sir, you have just refused the Sacrament of the Protestant Church; will you receive that of the Catholic?' and Charles replied 'Ah, I would give everything in the world to have a priest!'[8] But how to get a priest to Charles? The room was full of nosy onlookers. Could Barillon ask for a private audience or perhaps Catherine could? But there was no time and Catherine was unable. She did however have her own priests in close proximity to her chambers. James cleared the room telling the gathered men that the king required everyone but Lord Bath and Lord Feversham to retire.

Father Huddleston from Catherine's chapel at Somerset House was smuggled into the ruelle or recess beside the king's bed. In his own words published later the priest 'presented His Majesty with what services…(he) could perform for God's honour and the happiness of his soul at the last hour, on which eternity depends. The King then declared that he desired to die in the faith and communion of the Holy Roman Catholic Church…'[9]

Huddleston was then smuggled down the secret stairway that led from Charles' chambers and returned in secrecy to Somerset House. The king's rooms were opened again to his court and Catherine rushed to his side. She knelt by his bed in tears and begged him to forgive her for any offence she may have caused him. Charles told her that she 'had offended in nothing, but that he had been guilty of many offences against her, and he desired her pardon'.[10] Catherine collapsed with grief and her physicians took her back to her rooms. The Duke of York stayed with his brother throughout the night and the king's illegitimate children were brought in to say their goodbyes. Charles, knowing the end was near, made James promise to look after them as well as his past mistress the Lady Castlemaine (who had returned to England) and his current mistress Louise, Duchess of Portsmouth not to mention not allowing poor Nell Gwyn to starve. As a new day dawned Charles asked that the curtains be opened so that he could see the sun one last time and on that day 6th February 1685 around 11am he slipped away. The official cause of death was apoplexy or a stroke although rumour mongers did their best to spread gossip that he had been poisoned.

Catherine had been married to the English king for nearly twenty-three years. She had suffered his mistresses, been unable to have his children, was implicated in plots and accused of trying to kill him but she had never wavered in her affection for him and he had always been protective of her. Catherine knew that that protection had now gone and as she heard the heralds crying out 'The King is dead – long live the King!' she wondered what James' reign would have in store for her – but for now she must steel herself to listen to the condolences of the court. Her chambers were covered in black; floors, ceilings, walls and windows. By candlelight she received them on a bed of mourning including the new King James II. Here she read the letters too sent by other heads of state and her brother Pedro with whom she arranged to have masses sung in Lisbon on the anniversary of Charles' death for as long as she lived.

And Charles needed to be buried – a disconcerting dilemma for the new king. Charles had converted on his death bed and a Protestant funeral would not now be appropriate but Charles' conversion wasn't public knowledge and he also could not have the funeral conducted by Catholic priests. In the end it was a private affair. Charles was buried on the 14th of February at midnight in Westminster Abbey with Prince George of Denmark as chief mourner accompanied by the Privy Council and members of the royal household.

James began his reign by honouring his promise to look after Charles' mistresses. Nell received a pension of £1500 per year, the Duchess of Richmond £2000 and the Duchess of Portsmouth £3000. Catherine was granted a yearly allowance of £6000 in June along with other grants and income from her dower lands amounting to around £50,000 a year. Whilst for Catherine, Nell and Frances, England was their home for Louise it was just a matter of time before she returned to France.

Catherine stayed on in Whitehall for two months before returning to Somerset House in April where she put the Earl of Feversham in charge of her household. The Earl was a French Huguenot who had come to England in 1663. He had served as Master of the Horse and Lord Chamberlain to the queen but had become one of Charles most trusted Lords of the Bedchamber and was present at his death bed conversion. Now rumours started that he and Catherine were lovers and he was laughingly referred to as the king dowager.

Catherine had never taken a lover and she wasn't about to now. James and his wife Mary Beatrice were crowned king and queen on 23rd April. She would do nothing to upset her relationship with them. They were frequent visitors to Somerset House but Catherine was aware that her position was precarious. She did her best to improve their relationship especially cultivating her friendship with Mary Beatrice. When she had married James, Mary had been granted St James Chapel currently being used by Catherine and she had refused to part with it. Now the new Queen-Dowager made a gift of the chapel to the queen and they were joined in their devotions, publicly allowed to attend Catholic mass.

King James thoughts turned to those who had suffered because of the tumultuous years of the Popish Plot. He had the

Catholic Lords who remained in the Tower released and had Titus Oates, Catherine's old enemy, re-tried and convicted for perjury. Oates was fined 1000 marks, stripped of his clerical robes, sentenced to life imprisonment and a yearly punishment of being pilloried and whipped. It was an unusual judgement but there was no death penalty for perjury and perhaps his prosecutors hoped that his punishment would be the end of him. They certainly tried by making his castigation as severe as possible. On the day after his trial he was put in the pillory at Westminster and a crowd of 10,000 gathered to see him. Although many pelted him with eggs, there were also those who wished to save him. Before the mob grew angry, he was taken back to prison but brought out again to be whipped from Aldgate to Newgate by the king's executioner. He had one days' respite and then was whipped so severely from Newgate that 'he was dragged most of the way to Tyburn unconscious on a sled'[11] before being thrown back into prison to await his punishment the following year.

As those had conspired against him, now James faced the first threat to his succession but one he was well aware of. James called on Catherine to require the Earl of Feversham's services in June when Charles' errant son, the Duke of Monmouth returned from Holland to lead a rebellion to take the crown. Monmouth and his men landed at Lyme Regis, gathering troops as they made their way to Bristol. Feversham and Churchill headed the king's army sent to quell them. After chasing Monmouth across Somerset, where at Taunton he had himself crowned, the deciding battle was fought at Sedgemoor.

Feversham was triumphant. Five hundred of Monmouth's men were captured but the duke escaped aiming for the coast. The Royal Navy had already taken command of his ships and so he headed for Hampshire but at Ringwood he was captured.

Monmouth wrote to Catherine from there on 9th July.

Being in this unfortunate condition, and having non left but your majesty, that I think may have some compasion of me; and that, for the last king's sake, makes me take this boldnes to beg of you to interted for me. I would not desire your majestie to doe it, if I wear not, from the botom of my hart, convinced how I have bine disceaved into it, and how angry God Almighty is with me for it; but I hope, madam, your intersesian will give me life to repent of it, and to show the king (James II.) how reuly and truly I will serve him hearafter; and I hope, madam, your majesty will be convinced that the life you save will ever be devoted to your service, for I have been, and ever shall be, your majesty's most dutiful and obedient servant[12]

Catherine rushed to Whitehall to plead with James to spare Monmouth's life. She had ever been like a mother to Charles' illegitimate children and had frequently interceded for leniency when it came to Charles' eldest son but this time Monmouth had gone too far and his father was no longer alive to save him. Although Catherine convinced James to meet with Monmouth, it was to no avail. He was executed for treason on 15th July at Tower Hill. The men that had followed him were tried at the Bloody Assizes that started in Winchester and progressed through the West Country. Over 300 people were executed and a further 800 were sentenced to be transported to the West Indies.

In the autumn, Catherine became ill with the strain of it all. She told Pedro:

I was in bed having been there for twelve days, so ill with pain that was so strong and continuous that after groaning and perspiring for three or four hours without its diminishing, but increasing, I sent for one of the priests, being persuaded my hour had come. When he was at my bedside, God be praised! At that time the pain began to lessen, which I impute to a little oil which I have from the lamp of the Immaculate Conception of the Blessed Virgin of the town of Viçosa, which on occasion of my quinsy at three years of age, had the same effect. I continue somewhat better, though far from being well, since I am so devoted to my bed that I cannot stay all day out of it, which is never my custom, without great necessity.[13]

Charles was gone and now so was his son. What would life hold for her now? England had changed for Catherine. She could no longer see her place in it. It was around this time that she thought of returning to her beloved Portugal.

Chapter Ten

The Final Years
1686–1705

The next two years passed quietly until Catherine saw an opportunity to return to her native land. She needed both a ship and her brother Pedro's permission. Pedro's wife had died in 1683 and now he had found a new bride Princess Maria Sophia of Neuberg whom he married by proxy on 2nd July 1687. Her father Philip William, Elector Palatine, had contacted Catherine for help with the new bride's travel arrangements to Portugal and Catherine received James's permission for an English convoy to sail with the princess to Lisbon, stopping at Portsmouth en route. This was her chance and she wrote to Pedro immediately. She started emotionally:

> ...I live alone because it is suitable for me, as most people judge since the loss of the King (God rest his soul!), and on any disturbance occurring here either by death of the other (James) or during his life, as I have lost the King, I must look about for help here. My disease increases with time; and this being the case, I clearly perceive, it is very natural to try to stop this misfortune, and means are allowable for this purpose...

After reminding Pedro of her ill health, loneliness and precarious position, she told him:

> ...The present opportunity is very favourable, as the Elector Palatine wrote to me and asked that I should request a fleet of the King, my brother-in-law, for the conveyance of the Queen of Portugal, my much-loved sister. My great desire to see you makes this opportunity seem very suitable. I hope it may seem to you as

suitable as it does to me, and if I am to be as happy as I might be, do let me know immediately that you will not delay my great joy an instant longer than necessary. Remember how many years I have suffered, and if you decide not to make me so happy, give me a reason, in order that all may not vanish. I shall see the Queen here, since she is to pass our door in English ships. Since there is already a public rumour of our meeting, I pray you consider with all your judgment and good will how well I deserve of you, and if you wish not to make me happy by consenting that I should see you, which is all I desire, my reply is that there are here dissensions, changes, and even risks to life, what part of the world is more proper to me than my own country, where I have a brother for my prince and friend? If you deny this, look where else I may seek protection?...[1]

But Catherine's most heartfelt pleas fell on deaf ears. Pedro was caught up in his coming marriage and must have felt that Catherine was in no danger for the present time. Princess Maria arrived in Lisbon on 12th August 1687 without even meeting Catherine and was formally married to Pedro by the Archbishop of Lisbon at the Ribeira Palace on the same day. Catherine refused to give up and wrote letter after letter to Pedro, not always reminding him she wanted to come home, but keeping their communication open so that if another opportunity arose, he would remember her wishes. She was saddened that he ignored her pleas to return but as she had done with so many disappointments that she had experienced in her marriage, she stoically pressed on and there were financial matters to attend to.

Nell Gwyn died on 14th November 1687 at the young age of thirty-seven in the house Charles had given her in Pall Mall. She had suffered two strokes during the year and had never fully recovered. Catherine made sure her surviving son, Charles, did not slip into poverty by granting him a yearly pension of £2000 but it was time her own finances were put in order so that she could return to Portugal with a tidy sum when the opportunity arose. Catherine felt that the Lord Treasurer, Henry Hyde, the 2nd Earl of Clarendon, had withheld £36,000 due to her and in January 1688 she brought a law suit against him. It was a drastic move and not like Catherine. She was always so amenable and eager to find a simple solution but she needed the funds and wished to leave England with her monies intact.

Clarendon was appalled at Catherine's treatment of him and sought King James' counsel. James told him 'that he was ashamed of the queen-dowager's proceedings, but he could not interfere with the law, which he understood not, or control his law officers in what they deemed proper for his interests. As to the queen-dowager, she was a hard woman to deal with, and that she already knew his opinion of this suit'.[2] The court was dismayed that Catherine would use the law instead of coming to an amicable agreement but the Queen-Dowager felt she was in the right and the case would continue over many months.

The king had been shocked to hear that Catherine wanted to return to Portugal. He had thought her happy and content and took it personally she would want to leave but agreed to provide her with a vessel come the time of her departure. She had to wait for Pedro to send an ambassador to accompany her so although she would not be leaving anytime soon, she could make plans. She asked Manoel Diaz to liaise with her brother regarding the arrangements especially where she might live once she arrived in her home country – perhaps a farm or country house, somewhere that would be good for her health. As letters passed between the two courts, Pedro sent the aged Count of Ponteval to escort her home and James for his part journeyed to Chatham to choose the ships that would convey her to Portugal.

But Catherine then became extremely ill with a growth on her breast and was told by her physicians that travelling was out of the question. She wrote to Pedro:

I hope you are just enough to consider the pain with which I write this, since it is only in order to tell you that I cannot possibly make my journey with the great speed which my wish intended...[3]

And later when she had begun to recover she wrote again:

Thank God, for three days I have felt rather better, though it is so little that at times the pain begins to return to me again, which makes me believe that my bosom will fester again, as it has already done, and this is more painful for being internal.[4]

For now Catherine would have to postpone her homecoming. She was still ill when James had need of her in June to witness the birth of his son. To allay any suspicions around the birth of his child, the Queen-Dowager was requested to be at Queen Mary Beatrice's side throughout her delivery. She sat in a chair of state covered with a canopy by her bedside to watch, along with other witnesses including Frances Stuart, the Duchess of Richmond, the birth of a Catholic heir to the throne. Up until now James eldest daughter the protestant Mary who had married William of Orange was next in line to the throne. None of the duke's sons had survived much beyond infancy and rumours abounded that this new baby had been slipped into the bedchamber in a warming pan whilst his wife's stillborn child was removed.

In October Catherine stood as godmother and a few days later was called in front of the Privy Council to testify 'The king sent for me to the queen's labour. I came as soon as I could, and never left her till she was delivered of the prince of Wales'.[5] Her words were noted and she added her signature for proof. The other ladies present also testified. James was taking no chances his child wouldn't be seen as his rightful heir but his enemies were stacking against him.

William, Prince of Orange arrived early in November 1688 at Brixham near Torbay in Devon after receiving a formal invitation from the 'Immortal Seven' – a group of Protestant nobles – to invade England. Both William and Mary had doubts around the birth of James' new son and his right to succeed his father. The people as well were dissatisfied with James. They had never wanted a Catholic king and now they clamoured to welcome the Protestant prince.

The king knew that the tide was turning against him and tried to appeal to his daughter Mary to stop William's invasion. In October he had written to her 'And though I know you are a good wife, and ought to be so, yet for the same reason I must believe you will be still as good a daughter to a father that has always loved you so tenderly, and that has ever done the least thing to make you doubt it...'[6] Queen Mary Beatrice had also added 'I don't believe you could have such a thought against the worst of fathers, much less perform it against the best, that has always been kind to you, and I believe has loved you better than all the rest of his children'.[7] But it was no good appealing to Mary, who had never wanted to marry William, but was now completely loyal to him. Even Anne, the King's second eldest daughter, supported the prince.

As William's army of 11,000 foot men and 4,000 horse began to make its way to London, King James planned his escape. Already Queen Mary Beatrice had fled to France with their new son and he attempted to follow her but was captured by fishermen and returned to London under Dutch guard. On his way back into the city James was allowed to see Catherine at Somerset House. Her lord chamberlain, Feversham, had been sent by the king to William with a letter requesting they meet but poor Feversham had been arrested for his troubles. Catherine was appalled by his treatment. He had ever been faithful to her.

When William entered the city he called on her and found her sitting alone. He is reported to have asked her why she wasn't enjoying a game of basset to which she replied she couldn't do since she felt the absence of her Lord Chamberlain and 'he always kept the bank'.[8] William obligingly allowed his release.

And James was also allowed to 'escape' for a second time in December and this time he made it to France. With James gone, William and Mary could become the new king and queen of England.

On 13 February the royal couple formally accepted the crown and on the 11th April William and Mary were crowned as joint sovereigns in Westminster Abbey. James sent his daughter a note before her coronation 'I have been willing to overlook what has been done, and thought your obedience to your husband and compliance to the nation might have prevailed. But your being crowned is in your own power; if you do it while I and the Prince of Wales are living, the curses of an angry father will fall on you, as well as those of a God who commands obedience to parents'.[9] The note was subsequently destroyed and Mary may never have even read it. In any case the situation had gone too far now. It mattered not what her father thought. Mary was the new Queen of England.

Catherine didn't attend the coronation. She was keeping a low profile at Somerset House. The streets were dangerous for Catholics once more and Catherine was the last royal Catholic to remain in England. Pedro suggested that it was really time for her to come home regardless of whether she was still waiting on monies owed her. He said:

I have already told your majesty what could be done to secure the payment of what is promised to you, and that if they did not fulfil their engagements completely Your Majesty would come to Portugal, because there it would be possible for me to assist you. I now tell Your majesty the same thing, and it is a thing to consider, when in this kingdom they banish their King as a Catholic, and the man governs who, on pretence of destroying the Catholics, overthrows the foundations of sovereignty, ruining the holy Churches, and affecting the Catholics so that they seek other lands in order to free themselves, those who are not Catholics remaining there as in a safe home – how will it seem to the world, at the same time that all these things are known, to see that Your Majesty does not leave England?[10]

Catherine wanted to leave but how would she get home? Pedro urged her to return but where were the ships to take her? The country was in disarray and so she wrote to him 'No one can do anything until things here have run their course. The more knowledge I have the more I see that I can do nothing but withdraw while these things are settled'.[11]

In July a bill was passed against papists in the House of Commons and this reduced the number of servants Catherine could have to eighteen. The Lords did not support it but Catherine had no choice but to live with a smaller household. She decided to move to Islington and told Pedro 'My news is not what you desire, since my health is very poor and my happiness much diminished, and nothing else can be expected when the church is so oppressed as it is here at present. This grief, with the continual fear of invasion, causes me to live in little comfort, and thus I submit to live outside London, in a very small house hardly sufficient for a workman'.[12]

She had rented three cottages from an apothecary where the apartments for her servants were nothing more than cupboards and alcoves but she had a garden and she took some pleasure in walking there and making weekly visits to her chapel in London. She bombarded Pedro with letters, often repeating herself, but assuring him her thoughts these days were concentrated on how to get home. When Catherine heard that English ships were to escort the Princess Maria Anna of Neuberg to her marriage in Spain, she asked William for permission to join them but he refused. And again she wrote to Pedro, her lifeline, and told him 'I have begged ships of the King and he answered that it was impossible, and that he could not give them to me at present. It is certain that he gives them to your sister-in-law, Queen of

Castile...'[13] but not to Catherine.

She returned to Somerset House in October but in matter of days she received information that her palace was to be searched. The Earl of Shrewsbury had supposedly received news that arms and treasonable papers were concealed in the lodgings of one of Catherine's servants in Somerset House Yard. He had a warrant to search her home also looking for two popish priests who were supposedly hiding there. Nothing was found but it scared Catherine enough to ask Pedro to send one of his own ships for her. The seas at this time were being patrolled by nations at war and there was no way Pedro was going to chance his ship or his sister. Catherine would have to bide her time a while longer.

In March 1690 the deposed King James II landed in Ireland with a French invasion force and by June, William of Orange was preparing to meet him. Catherine was surprised to receive a visit from Lord Nottingham with a message from William before he left to tell her 'that it was observed there were great meetings and caballings against his government at her residence of Somerset House, he therefore desired that her majesty would please to leave town, and take up her abode at either Windsor or Audley End'.[14] She had been living quietly at her London residence, not troubling any one and only asking that she could return to her former country. Now the new king was trying to get her to leave the only place she felt safe. Her response to Nottingham was that she would rather go to Portugal if ships could be arranged for her voyage. She had asked before and if he truly wanted her to leave well then arrange that departure and all would be well. Nottingham slunk away.

Not at all happy Catherine sent Lords Feversham and Halifax to William the next day to make her case. Her reply came in the form of Nottingham again who appeared the next evening to tell her she needn't move after all. Catherine couldn't fathom what that episode had really been about but she was soon to realise that it was Mary who bore her a grudge and was behind

William's order and her mistreatment.

After the king had left for Ireland, Queen Mary ordered prayers to be said in all the churches of England for his success. But for William's success, it meant James would fail. The Savoy Chapel was attached to Somerset House for Protestant worship. Catherine never went there but her servants did. Whether she specifically ordered the prayer not to be said or whether it was just omitted, it was nevertheless left out and Mary was furious. The chaplain was arrested and severely questioned. Shaking with fear, he told the Privy Council that Lord Feversham had given him orders not to read the prayer and he feared if he had that Catherine might stop all further services in the chapel. Feversham took the blame, begging the queen's pardon which she refused to give because the issue concerned the person of the king and she didn't believe Catherine's Lord Chamberlain either. Mary thought 'no more measures ought to be kept with the Queen-Dowager after this, if it were her order, which no doubt it was'[15] and she geared up for an argument with Catherine when she attended court. But Catherine would not be drawn into a spat with James's eldest daughter and Mary wrote to William that the Queen-Dowager 'did not stay a moment, nor say two words'[16] on her next visit to court.

Catherine had had enough and she asked permission to travel to Hamburg but with French ships patrolling the coast it was too dangerous. Then she decided she would go to Bath but Mary was loath to provide her with guards. So in July Catherine decided to stay with the nuns she patronised in Hammersmith before going on to Windsor. Infuriatingly, Mary ordered that she close her Catholic chapel at Somerset House – something that she had never been forced to do even at the height of the Popish Plot. However Mary goaded Catherine, the Queen-Dowager remained courteous to her. The child who she had once comforted after her mother's death and whom she had tried to help when she was so petrified at her marriage had turned against her as a woman.

Catherine couldn't fathom it and no longer did she care.

Catherine found no solace at Windsor. She paced the halls where she and Charles had spent many a summer and walked in the park as she had once done with the king. Life with Charles had never been easy but here they had shared pleasant, companionable times. What peace she found was broken by hearing a rumour that she was now trying to poison Queen Mary and so she journeyed back to Somerset House. William was due to return victorious from his battles in Ireland and she could begin once more to harry him for permission to go home. But it would be more than another year before she finally got the permission she so long sought.

Eventually however, on 30th March 1692, the gates of Somerset House were opened to a procession of coaches carrying Catherine and her ladies including the Countess of Fingall and Lady Tuke, and over a hundred other servants. Catherine left Lord Feversham in charge of the house with £10,000 to pay those who stayed in England. The house was still hers and she felt responsible for those who had been loyal to her but now it really was time to get her return journey to Portugal under way.

Her coach was cheered on by a city crowd as she passed the Strand, Temple Bar and London Bridge. At the Tower of London, a gun salute sounded a goodbye to the Queen-Dowager who had spent nearly thirty years in England. Catherine was nervous and excited about the journey ahead but she only got as far as Dover before complications arose. Ships were waiting to carry her, her entourage and their possessions to France but they needed to be accompanied by English men-of-war and Queen Mary delayed the order for her safe passage. Her last act of spite. Finally permission was given and Catherine sailed for Dieppe.

King Louis XIV provided Catherine with an escort through France. He invited her to stay awhile at the French court in Versailles but she was anxious to begin her travels through France and Spain. She asked instead that she be permitted to stop at Rouen, Saint-Germain-en-Laye and take the waters at Bourbon. The deposed King James was living in Saint-Germain but was away with his army so Catherine spent a few hours with Mary Beatrice talking of old times. After Bourbon, Catherine continued on to Lyon and was in Avignon by the end of September. The Duke of Grammont met her at Bayonne and escorted her to the Spanish border where she gave him a diamond worth ten thousand *écus* for his troubles. She was now met by her brother's escort and hoped to travel swiftly through Spain but within days she was struck down with erysipelas, a debilitating skin condition combined with a fever, and was so ill she had to stay in Matapozuelos near Valladolid for weeks. She wrote to Pedro 'I pray you have a little patience until I am stronger, since the light is troublesome to my eyes, and my hand and arm tremble so that I cannot hold a pen in my hand'.[17] Spain's court physician, Antonio Mendes, was called for but it was some time before Catherine recovered.

She finally crossed the border to Almeida at the end of December. It had been a long and tiring journey but Catherine was overjoyed to be back in Portugal. Her illness forgotten she travelled on to the capital of Lisbon where a state welcome awaited her. The people of Lisbon cheered and waved, scattering flower petals in front of her carriages, glad to see their once princess return. Pedro drove out to meet her and after a dignified and formal welcome she joined him in his coach to retire to the Quinta of Alcantara, a pleasure palace outside the town where apartments had been made ready for her and Pedro's queen, Maria Sophia was waiting to greet her. Formalities over Catherine could retire but not for long. The following days were filled with banquets in her honour and celebrations to attend. Her heart was gladdened and her friendship with Maria Sophia blossomed. Her relationship with Pedro however was not so relaxed.

Catherine had become too anglicised for his tastes and he

frowned on her English mode of dress. Where once as a princess arriving in England, she had been frowned upon for wearing stiff and formal Portuguese clothes now she was being admonished for the more scandalous necklines and bare arms shown by her English dresses. Catherine refused to return to the traditional dresses of her home country and she found support from Queen Maria Sophia and the ladies of the court who also wanted to be wearing something more fashionable. Pedro was petitioned and although displeased the ladies won his permission to send to France for new tailors.

Catherine now made the most of being back in Portugal and she travelled around for the next few years staying at the quintas in the Conde de Redonda near Santa Martha then the Conde de Aveiras at Belem. In February 1699, she stayed at her birth place, the Villa Viçosa and made a state visit to Evora. It was her version of a progress where she could meet the people and reacquaint herself with the country of her birth.

She returned to Lisbon when she heard of Queen Maria Sophia's death in August 1699 but was soon off on her travels again. In May 1700 she decided to settle back at court with plans to move to her new residence of Bemposta Palace as soon as it was finished. Building had begun in 1694 but there was still more to do to make the palace fit for the Queen-Dowager including having the arms of England prominently displayed over its great doors.

As she remembered them, the English still remembered her including the infamous Pepys who had finished writing his diaries by now due to poor eyesight. He wrote a letter to his nephew John when he heard he was in Portugal:

If this should find you in Lisbon, I give you in charge to wait upon my Lady Tuke, one of the ladies attending my once royal mistress, our Queen-Dowager, a lady for whom I bear great honour; nor if she should offer you the honour of kissing the Queen's hand would I have you to omit, if Lady Tuke thinks it proper, the presenting her majesty with my profoundest duty, as becomes a most faithful subject[18]

Catherine kept in touch with news from England including Queen Mary of England's death in 1694 and Hortense Mancini's death in 1699. Evelyn recorded at the time:

Now died the famous Duchess of Mazarin. She had been the richest lady in Europe; she was niece to Cardinal Mazarin, and was married to the richest subject in Europe, as was said; she was born at Rome, educated in France, and was an extraordinary beauty and wit, but dissolute, and impatient of matrimonial restraint, so as to be abandoned by her husband, and banished: when she came to England for shelter, lived on a pension given her here, and is reported to have hastened her death by intemperate drinking strong spirits.[19]

When James II died in September 1701, Catherine ordered Somerset House to be hung in black and sent word that all her servants that remained there wear mourning dress for a year. Many of her English ladies had returned home and these days she kept a smaller household with Portuguese ladies of high birth. Catherine, now in her sixties, had outlived many of the people who had taken a part in her life.

In March 1702, William of Orange died and James's daughter Anne succeeded to the throne. Frances, Duchess of Richmond, had stayed in touch with Catherine over the years and she wrote to her to tell her of the new queen's coronation. But Frances herself was ailing and she died in October of the same year.

Catherine was happy enough to life a quiet and simple life in her final years. Her palace at Bemposta was ready for her and from here she could easily visit her brother and her nephews John, Francisco, Antonio and Manuel and her niece Francisca. In

April 1704, she had another serious attack of erysipelas which confined her to her bed just at a time when the young Charles of Austria, a claimant to the Spanish crown, wished to pay her a visit accompanied by his tutor. The court had to hurry over to Bemposta Palace to fill its walls and put on a show of magnificence as if Catherine was living surrounded by courtiers when in fact she kept as small a household as possible.

> *No one accompanied him to the chamber of the queen-dowager of England, save his tutor, who, having placed a chair of black velvet, which had been provided purposely for his use, at a convenient distance from the bed, withdrew, to wait at the door of the chamber, in the same apartment wherein all the ladies were assembled. Queen Catharine, in consequence of her severe indisposition, was in her bed. One lady only, donna Inez Antonia de Tavora, the lady-in-waiting for the week, was with her, serving at the foot of the bed, when the king of Spain entered, and as soon as lie prepared to sit down, she withdrew to the hall. The interview of their majesties being strictly private, nothing is known of what passed, beyond the elaborate compliments with which they met, and the formal courtesies that were exchanged when the royal visitor took his leave of the sick queen...*[20]

Catherine was aware of the war raging over the Spanish succession which had been fought since the death of the childless Charles II in 1700. Her visitor Charles had a claim to the throne but so did others and Portugal was divided by those who supported his claim and those who supported the French claim. It would become all the more important to Catherine when her brother fell ill. Given the political situation if Portugal was to lose its king it would be disastrous. Pedro's successor John was a teenager and too young to reign on his own. Pedro resisted appointing a regent until he became so ill he was thought close to death and received extreme unction. He recovered but retired to

Beira and named Catherine Queen Regent of Portugal in 1705.

Now Catherine came into her own power. The war of succession had escalated and it was time for Portugal to subdue French troops and assert Charles' right to the throne. Catherine directed the campaign with decisiveness and precision. She thought of everything from recruiting new men, organising their deployment and movements to providing food for them and the horses. She continually came up against opposition from the Duke of Cadaval and the Portuguese councillors who were negotiating with their allies in England and Holland but in the end Catherine's direction ensured the conquest of Valencia de Alcantara, Albuquerque, Salvaterra, and Carca. She had proved herself to be an effective, just and a triumphant ruler. For so long she been in Charles' shadow in England, in Portugal she was bathed in light.

Catherine's victories were short-lived however. She had thrived as her country's regent, her health had improved although she was now sixty-seven, but on 31st December she was suddenly gripped with acute stomach pains. By 10pm she was dead in her palace at Bemposta. No one had expected her death and shock waves carried the news around Lisbon.

After she had passed she lay on her death bed, with candles lit at her head and feet, and her councillors read out her will. Ever generous Catherine left one year's salary to all her servants and gave special endowments to those she favoured most. She provided for six convents as well as other religious houses and left dowries for six virgins to become nuns. Ten thousand cruzados were left to fund the nurses for abandoned children, six hundred milreis was left for the redemption of slaves with special thought that any young boys or girls amongst them be redeemed first. She even designated money for the freedom of petty debtors.

Catherine had wanted to be buried at Belem monastery, built on the spot from which Vasco de Gama had sailed on his voyage of discovery, along with her brothers who had predeceased her and her wishes were honoured for her final journey. Her people lined the way from Bemposta Palace to the monastery where she was interred with all the funeral rites due her station. Lisbon closed down for eight days and for a year afterwards the court stayed in mourning for their princess, their Queen Regent and the Queen-Dowager of England, Charles II's restoration queen.

Afterword

Catherine has largely been a forgotten queen marked by history as the neglected wife of Charles II and not much more. Charles II's court is remembered for its debauchery and licentiousness and the king himself for his many mistresses. Catherine however lived amongst them and with her strength of character retained her piety and devotion. She deserves credit for maintaining her position against all the odds and coming into her own as queen regent of Portugal in her later years.

Catherine had no children to continue her line but she is still remembered by some today. In 1839, a series of paintings were discovered in a house in Sandwich that depicted a royal visit to the Kentish town in 1672. Amongst them are four depictions of Catherine's state entry into the town and three quarter length life-size portraits of Catherine, Charles and the Duke of York painted by William Van der Velde, a Dutch artist. They were donated to the town council and can be viewed in the council chamber at Sandwich's Guildhall.

She is also remembered by the Queen's Royal Surrey Regiment. The regiment first served in Tangier, given to England as part of Catherine's dowry. Their role was to defend the town from constant attack from the Moors until 1684 when Charles withdrew his troops and the regiment returned home to be granted the title of the Queen-Dowager's Regiment of Foot after his death in 1685. At the time they used the symbol of the Paschal lamb, associated with the House of Braganza, on their regimental badges. The regiment's history is a long and varied one but in Catherine's time they fought at the Battle of Sedgemoor chasing down the errant Duke of Monmouth, Charles' son, and also served in Ireland under King William.

Some historians also believe that Queens in New York was named for Catherine as one of the twelve original counties of

New York. Yet a long running dispute about her role or more pertinently the Stuart link to the slave trade compromised a project to place a 33ft tall statue of her by the Hudson river. Instead a smaller version of the statue now stands facing the Tagus River and looks towards New York in the Parque do Tejo, Lisbon.

Nowhere is Catherine remembered more than in her home country of Portugal.

References

Chapter One

1. Mackay, *Catherine of Braganza*
2. Davidson, *Catherine of Braganca*
3. Ibid.
4. Strickland, *Lives of the Queens of England*
5. CSP, Venice
6. CSP, Venice
7. Mackay, *Catherine of Braganza*
8. Jordan, *The King's Bed: Sex, Power and the Court of Charles II*
9. Hyde, *The Life of Edward, Earl of Clarendon*
10. Davidson, *Catherine of Braganca*
11. Ibid.
12. Ibid.
13. Strickland, *Lives of the Queens of England*
14. Mackay, *Catherine of Braganza*
15. Pepys, *The Diary of Samuel Pepys*
16. Strickland, *Lives of the Queens of England*
17. Ibid.
18. Wilson, *Love in Letters*
19. Mackay, *Catherine of Braganza*
20. Hartman, *La Belle Stuart*
21. Davidson, *Catherine of Braganca*
22. Iter Lusitania; or the Portugal Voyage poem 1662 quoted in Strickland, *Lives of the Queens of England*
23. Ibid.
24. Pepys, *The Diary of Samuel Pepys*
25. Hyde, *The Life of Edward, Earl of Clarendon*
26. Pepys, *The Diary of Samuel Pepys*
27. CSP, Venice
28. Howitt, *Biographical Sketches of the Queens of Great Britain*
29. Burnet, *History of His Own Times*

30. Mackay, *Catherine of Braganza*
31. Norrington, *My Dearest Minette: letters between Charles II and his sister, the Duchesse d'Orleans*

Chapter Two

1. Pepys, *The Diary of Samuel Pepys*
2. Strickland, *Lives of the Queens of England*
3. Davidson, *Catherine of Braganca*
4. Evelyn, *The Diary of John Evelyn*
5. Ibid.
6. Stratton Holloway, *American Furniture and Decoration Colonial and Federal*
7. Pepys, *The Diary of Samuel Pepys*
8. CSP, Venice
9. Ibid.
10. Melville, *The Windsor Beauties: Ladies of the Court of Charles II*
11. Hyde, *The Life of Edward, Earl of Clarendon*
12. Ibid.
13. Ibid.
14. Ibid.
15. Norrington, *My Dearest Minette: letters between Charles II and his sister, the Duchesse d'Orleans*
16. Davidson, *Catherine of Braganca*
17. Strickland, *Lives of the Queens of England*
18. Plowden, *Henrietta Maria: Charles I's Indomitable Queen*
19. Strickland, *Lives of the Queens of England*
20. Evelyn, *The Diary of John Evelyn*
21. Pepys, *The Diary of Samuel Pepys*
22. Ibid.
23. Hamilton, *The Illustrious Lady*
24. Strickland, *Lives of the Queens of England*
25. Ibid.
26. Ibid.
27. Hyde, *The Life of Edward, Earl of Clarendon*

28. Whittingham, C, (ed.) *The British Poets*
29. Mackay, *Catherine of Braganza*
30. Pepys, *The Diary of Samuel Pepys*
31. Norrington, *My Dearest Minette: letters between Charles II and his sister, the Duchesse d'Orleans*
32. Pepys, *The Diary of Samuel Pepys*
33. Davidson, *Catherine of Braganca*
34. Pepys, *The Diary of Samuel Pepys*
35. Ibid.
36. Hargrave, *Complete Collection of State Trials*
37. Ibid.
38. Hartman, *La Belle Stuart*
39. Pepys, *The Diary of Samuel Pepys*
40. Davidson, *Catherine of Braganca*
41. Pepys, *The Diary of Samuel Pepys*
42. Norrington, *My Dearest Minette: letters between Charles II and his sister, the Duchesse d'Orleans*
43. Pepys, *The Diary of Samuel Pepys*
44. Strickland, *Lives of the Queens of England*
45. Whittingham, C. (ed.) *The British Poets*
46. Norrington, *My Dearest Minette: letters between Charles II and his sister, the Duchesse d'Orleans*
47. Hamilton, *The Illustrious Lady*
48. Ibid.
49. Pepys, *The Diary of Samuel Pepys*
50. Strickland, *Lives of the Queens of England*
51. Ibid.

Chapter Three

1. Pepys, *The Diary of Samuel Pepys*
2. Ibid.
3. Norrington, *My Dearest Minette: letters between Charles II and his sister, the Duchesse d'Orleans*
4. Davidson, *Catherine of Braganca*

5. Calendar of State Papers, domestic
6. Pepys, *The Diary of Samuel Pepys*
7. Ibid.
8. Ibid.
9. Strickland, *Lives of the Queens of England*
10. Uglow, *A Gambling Man: Charles II and the Restoration*
11. Evelyn, *The Diary of John Evelyn*
12. Hanson, *The Great Fire of London*
13. Wilson, *All the King's Women: Love, sex and politics in the life of Charles II*
14. Mackay, *Catherine of Braganza*
15. Pepys, *The Diary of Samuel Pepys*

Chapter Four

1. Strickland, *Lives of the Queens of England*
2. Pepys, *The Diary of Samuel Pepys*
3. Norrington, *My Dearest Minette: letters between Charles II and his sister, the Duchesse d'Orleans*
4. Hopkins, *Constant Delights: Rakes, rogues and scandal in Restoration England*
5. Strickland, *Lives of the Queens of England*
6. Evelyn, *The Diary of John Evelyn*
7. Strickland, *Lives of the Queens of England*
8. Pepys, *The Diary of Samuel Pepys*
9. Burnet, *History of His Own Times*
10. Ibid.
11. Strickland, *Lives of the Queens of England*
12. *The Poor Whores Petition*
13. Norrington, *My Dearest Minette: letters between Charles II and his sister, the Duchesse d'Orleans*
14. Ibid.
15. Pepys, *The Diary of Samuel Pepys*
16. Goodwin, *Memoirs of Count Grammont by Count Anthony Hamilton*

17. Pepys, *The Diary of Samuel Pepys*
18. Norrington, *My Dearest Minette: letters between Charles II and his sister, the Duchesse d'Orleans*
19. Davidson, *Catherine of Braganca*
20. Wilson, *Nell Gwyn: Royal Mistress*

Chapter Five

1. Mackay, *Catherine of Braganza*
2. Norrington, *My Dearest Minette: letters between Charles II and his sister, the Duchesse d'Orleans*
3. Jordan, *The King's Bed: Sex, Power and the Court of Charles II*
4. Beauclerk, *Nell Gwyn: A Biography*
5. Ibid.
6. Davidson, *Catherine of Braganca*
7. Burnet, *History of His Own Times*
8. Strickland, *Lives of the Queens of England*
9. Hopkins, *Constant Delights: Rakes, rogues and scandal in Restoration England*
10. Quoted in Strickland, *Lives of the Queens of England*
11. Ibid.
12. Strickland, *Lives of the Queens of England*
13. Mackay, *Catherine of Braganza*
14. Bevan, *Charles the Second's French Mistress*

Chapter Six

1. Wilson, *All the King's Women: Love, sex and politics in the life of Charles II*
2. Calendar of State papers, Domestic
3. Ibid.
4. Evelyn, *The Diary of John Evelyn*
5. Halstead, *Richard III as Duke of Gloucester and King of England*
6. Wilson, *All the King's Women: Love, sex and politics in the life of Charles II*
7. Bevan, *Charles the Second's French Mistress*

8. Evelyn, *The Diary of John Evelyn*
9. Bevan, *Charles the Second's French Mistress*
10. Waller, *The Triple Combat*
11. Goodwin, *Memoirs of Count Grammont by Count Anthony Hamilton*
12. Bevan, *Charles the Second's French Mistress*
13. Ibid.
14. Mackay, *Catherine of Braganza*

Chapter Seven

1. Bevan, *Charles the Second's French Mistress*
2. Davidson, *Catherine of Braganca*
3. Fraser, *King Charles II*
4. Mackay, *Catherine of Braganza*
5. Davidson, *Catherine of Braganca*
6. Mackay, *Catherine of Braganza*
7. Calendar of State papers, Domestic
8. Ibid.
9. Strickland, *Lives of the Queens of England*
10. Evelyn, *The Diary of John Evelyn*
11. Mackay, *Catherine of Braganza*
12. Kenyon, *The Popish Plot*
13. Ibid.
14. Mackay, *Catherine of Braganza*
15. Ibid.
16. Ibid.
17. Ibid.
18. Ibid.
19. Kenyon, *The Popish Plot*
20. Hyde, *The Life of Edward, Earl of Clarendon*
21. Mackay, *Catherine of Braganza*

Chapter Eight

1. Merians, *The Secret Malady*

2. Wilson, *All the King's Women: Love, sex and politics in the life of Charles II*
3. Bevan, *Charles the Second's French Mistress*
4. Strickland, *Lives of the Queens of England*
5. Davidson, *Catherine of Braganca*
6. Ibid.
7. Strickland, *Lives of the Queens of England*
8. Evelyn, *The Diary of John Evelyn*
9. Ibid.
10. Strickland, *Lives of the Queens of England*
11. Mackay, *Catherine of Braganza*
12. Davidson, *Catherine of Braganca*
13. Bevan, *Charles the Second's French Mistress*
14. Ibid.
15. Evelyn, *The Diary of John Evelyn*
16. Beauclerk, *Nell Gwyn: A Biography*
17. Davidson, *Catherine of Braganca*
18. Quoted in Strickland, *Lives of the Queens of England*
19. Bucholz, *The Augustan Court: Queen Anne and the Decline of Court Culture*

Chapter Nine

1. Evelyn, *The Diary of John Evelyn*
2. Ibid.
3. Strickland, *Lives of the Queens of England*
4. Mackay, *Catherine of Braganza*
5. Fraser, *King Charles II*
6. Mackay, *Catherine of Braganza*
7. Davidson, *Catherine of Braganca*
8. Ibid.
9. Ibid.
10. Ibid.
11. Kenyon, *The Popish Plot*
12. *Original Letters Illustrative of English History*

13. Davidson, *Catherine of Braganca*

Chapter Ten

1. Davidson, *Catherine of Braganca*
2. Strickland, *Lives of the Queens of England*
3. Davidson, *Catherine of Braganca*
4. Ibid.
5. Strickland, *Lives of the Queens of England*
6. Kiste, *William and Mary*
7. Ibid.
8. Mackay, *Catherine of Braganza*
9. Kiste, *William and Mary*
10. Davidson, *Catherine of Braganza*
11. Mackay, *Catherine of Braganza*
12. Ibid.
13. Davidson, *Catherine of Braganca*
14. Strickland, *Lives of the Queens of England*
15. Davidson, *Catherine of Braganca*
16. Ibid.
17. Ibid.
18. Strickland, *Lives of the Queens of England*
19. Evelyn, *The Diary of John Evelyn*
20. Strickland, *Lives of the Queens of England*

Select Bibliography

Airy, Osmund, *Charles II*, London, 1904

Andrews, Allen, *The Royal Whore*, London, 1971

Ashley, Maurice, *The Stuarts In Love*, London, 1963

Beauclerk, Charles, *Nell Gwyn: A Biography*, London, 2005

Bevan, Bryan, *Charles the II's Minette*, London, 1979

Bevan, Bryan, *Charles the Second's French Mistress*, London, 1972

Bevan, Bryan, *The Duchess Hortense: Cardinal Mazarin's Wanton Niece,* London, 1987

Bryant, Arthur, *Restoration England*, London, 1960

Bucholz, R. O. *The Augustan Court: Queen Anne and the Decline of Court Culture*, California, 1993

Burnet, Gilbert, *History of His Own Times*, 6 vols, London, 1833

Calendar of State Papers, Domestic – Charles II

Calendar of State Papers, Venice

Chapman, Hester, *Mary II, Queen of England*, London, 1953

Davidson, Lillias Campbell, *Catherine of Braganca, Infanta of Portugal and Queen-Consort of England*, London, 1908

Elsna, Hebe, *Catherine of Braganza: Charles II's Queen*, London, 1967

Evelyn, John, *The Diary of John Evelyn*, (kindle edition) Los Angeles, 2009

Fraser, Antonia, *King Charles II*, London, 2002

Fraser, Antonia, *The Weaker Vessel*, London, 1984

Gilmour, Margaret, *The Great Lady – A biography of Barbara Villiers*, New York, 1941

Goodwin, Gordon (ed.) *Memoirs of Count Grammont by Count Anthony Hamilton*, Edinburgh, 1908

Graham, Hinds, Hobby & Wilcox (eds), *Her Own Life: autobiographical writings by seventeenth-century Englishwomen*, London, 1989

Haile, Martin, *Queen Mary of Modena: her life and letters*, London,

1905

Halstead, Caroline Amelia, *Richard III as Duke of Gloucester and King of England*, London, 1844

Hargrave, Francis (ed.) *Complete Collection of State Trials*, Volume 2, 1795

Hartman, Cyril Hughes, *La Belle Stuart*, London, 1924

Hartman, Cyril Hughes, *Charles II and Madame*, London, 1934

Hamilton, Elizabeth, *Henrietta Maria*, London, 1976

Hamilton, Elizabeth, *The Illustrious Lady*, London, 1980

Hanrahan, David, *Charles II and the Duke of Buckingham*, Stroud, 2006

Hanrahan, David, *Colonel Blood: The Man who Stole the Crown Jewels*, Stroud, 2004

Hanson, Neil, *The Great Fire of London*, New York, 2002

Hopkins, Graham, *Constant Delights: Rakes, rogues and scandal in Restoration England*, London, 2002

Hopkins, Graham, *Nell Gwynne – A Passionate Life*, London, 2000

Hopkirk, Mary, *Queen Over the Water, Mary Beatrice of Modena Queen of James II*, London, 1953

Howitt, Mary Botham, *Biographical Sketches of the Queens of Great Britain*, London, 1862

Hyde, Edward, *The Life of Edward, earl of Clarendon by himself*, 1761

Jordan D & Walsh M, *The King's Bed: Sex, Power and the Court of Charles II*, London, 2015

Kenyon, John, *The Popish Plot*, London, 1972

Kenyon, J P, *Stuart England*, London, 1978

Ollrad, Richard, *Clarendon and His Friends*, Oxford, 1987

Mackay, Janet, *Catherine of Braganza*, London, 1937

Marshall, Alan, *The Strange Death of Edmund Godfrey*, Stroud, 1999

Masters, Brian, *The Mistresses of Charles II*, London, 1979

Melville, Lewis, *The Windsor Beauties: Ladies of the Court of Charles II*, Michigan, 2005

Merians, Linda Evi, *The Secret Malady: Venereal Disease in Eighteenth-century Britain and France*, Kentucky, 1992

Norrington, Ruth, (ed.) *My Dearest Minette: letters between Charles II and his sister, the Duchesse d'Orleans*, London, 1996

Original Letters Illustrative of English History, London, 1824

Pepys, *The Diary of Samuel Pepys*, ed. Latham & Matthews, 11 vols, 1970–83

Plowden, Alison, *Henrietta Maria: Charles I's Indomitable Queen*, Stroud, 2001

Plowden, Alison, *The Stuart Princesses*, Stroud, 1996

Porter, Stephen, *Pepy's London*, Stroud, 2012

Pritchard, R E, *Scandalous Liaisons: Charles II and his Court*, Stroud, 2015

Spencer, Charles, *Prince Rupert: The Last Cavalier*, London, 2007

Stratton Holloway, Edward, *American Furniture and Decoration Colonial and Federal*, Read Books Ltd, 2013

Strickland, Agnes, *Lives of the Queens of England*, Vol VIII, 1851

The Poor Whores Petition, 1668

Thomas, Gertrude Z, *Richer Than Spices*, Toronto, 1965

Trevelyan, G M, *England Under the Stuarts*, London, 1904

Uglow, Jenny, *A Gambling Man: Charles II and the Restoration*, London, 2009

Van Der Kiste, John, *William and Mary*, Stroud, 2003

Waller, Edmund, *The Triple Combat*, 1675

Wheatley, Dennis, *Old Rowley: A Very Private Life of Charles II*, London, 1962

Whittingham, C, (ed), *The British Poets*, Chiswick, 1822

Wilson, Derek, *All the King's Women: Love, sex and politics in the life of Charles II*, London, 2003

Wilson, James Grant, *Love in Letters*, London, 1867

Wilson, John Harold, *Nell Gwyn: Royal Mistress*, New York, 1952

Chronos Books
HISTORY

Chronos Books is an historical non-fiction imprint. Chronos publishes real history for real people; bringing to life people, places and events in an imaginative, easy-to-digest and accessible way - histories that pass on their stories to a generation of new readers.
If you have enjoyed this book, why not tell other readers by posting a review on your preferred book site. Recent bestsellers from Chronos Books are:

Lady Katherine Knollys
The Unacknowledged Daughter of King Henry VIII

Sarah-Beth Watkins
A comprehensive account of Katherine Knollys' questionable paternity, her previously unexplored life in the Tudor court and her intriguing relationship with Elizabeth I.
Paperback: 978-1-78279-585-8 ebook: 978-1-78279-584-1

Cromwell was Framed
Ireland 1649

Tom Reilly
Revealed: The definitive research that proves the Irish nation owes Oliver Cromwell a huge posthumous apology for wrongly convicting him of civilian atrocities in 1649.
Paperback: 978-1-78279-516-2 ebook: 978-1-78279-515-5

Why The CIA Killed JFK and Malcolm X
The Secret Drug Trade in Laos

John Koerner
A new groundbreaking work presenting evidence that the CIA
silenced JFK to protect its secret drug trade in Laos.
Paperback: 978-1-78279-701-2 ebook: 978-1-78279-700-5

The Disappearing Ninth Legion
A Popular History

Mark Olly
The Disappearing Ninth Legion examines hard evidence for the
foundation, development, mysterious disappearance, or
possible continuation of Rome's lost Legion.
Paperback: 978-1-84694-559-5 ebook: 978-1-84694-931-9

Beaten But Not Defeated
Siegfried Moos - A German anti-Nazi who settled in Britain

Merilyn Moos
Siegi Moos, an anti-Nazi and active member of the German
Communist Party, escaped Germany in 1933 and, exiled in
Britain, sought another route to the transformation of
capitalism.
Paperback: 978-1-78279-677-0 ebook: 978-1-78279-676-3

A Schoolboy's Wartime Letters
An evacuee's life in WWII — A Personal Memoir

Geoffrey Iley
A boy writes home during WWII, revealing his own fascinating
story, full of zest for life, information and humour.
Paperback: 978-1-78279-504-9 ebook: 978-1-78279-503-2

The Life & Times of the Real Robyn Hoode
Mark Olly
A journey of discovery. The chronicles of the genuine historical
character, Robyn Hoode, and how he became one of England's
greatest legends.
Paperback: 978-1-78535-059-7 ebook: 978-1-78535-060-3

Readers of ebooks can buy or view any of these bestsellers by
clicking on the live link in the title. Most titles are published
in paperback and as an ebook. Paperbacks are available in
traditional bookshops. Both print and ebook formats are
available online.

Find more titles and sign up to our readers' newsletter at
http://www.johnhuntpublishing.com/history-home

Follow us on Facebook at
https://www.facebook.com/ChronosBooks

and Twitter at https://twitter.com/ChronosBooks